The Continental Commitment

Also by Michael Howard

THE FRANCO-PRUSSIAN WAR

THE MEDITERRANEAN STRATEGY
IN THE SECOND WORLD WAR

STUDIES IN WAR AND PEACE

GRAND STRATEGY, vol. IV:
AUGUST 1942–SEPTEMBER 1943
(*UK Official History of the Second World War,
Military Series*)

Edited by Michael Howard

SOLDIERS AND GOVERNMENTS

THE THEORY AND PRACTICE OF WAR

The Continental Commitment

The dilemma of British defence policy in the era of the two world wars . The Ford Lectures in the University of Oxford 1971

MICHAEL HOWARD

*Fellow of All Souls College, Oxford
and of the British Academy*

Temple Smith · London

First published in Great Britain 1972
by Maurice Temple Smith Ltd
37 Great Russell Street, London WC1
© 1972 MICHAEL HOWARD
ISBN 0 8511 7030 7
Printed in Great Britain by
Western Printing Services Ltd,
Bristol

Contents

Preface

These lectures are reprinted substantially as they were delivered at Oxford in the spring of 1971, with all the drawbacks that this involves; including the relegation of a certain amount of illustrative material to the footnotes. The time available for their preparation did not permit me to look further, in the official archives, than the records of the Cabinet and its relevant Committees, and at by no means all of these; or to use more than a tiny fraction of the private collections of papers now available. As a result the picture I have drawn is probably distorted and certainly incomplete. Scholars who have mastered the files of the Foreign Office and the Service Ministries will be appalled at my errors and superficialities.

None the less it seemed worth risking their strictures in order to attempt, even on the basis of so incomplete a study, a very rough preliminary sketch of British defence policy as it unfolded during the first half of the present century. I did not set out to prove any particular thesis, but during the course of my work a thesis has certainly emerged—and a somewhat controversial one at that. This should at least provide a starting point for further discussion and study of an inexhaustible subject.

I am grateful to the Warden and Fellows of New College, Oxford, for access to the Milner Papers in the Bodleian Library, Oxford; to Mr Mark Bonham-Carter for access to the Asquith Papers in the same repository; and to Mr Brian

Bond for access to the papers of the late Lieutenant General Sir Henry Pownall in his possession. Lord Esher kindly allowed me to quote from his grandfather's journals; Messrs Hutchinson from *My Political Life* by Mr L. S. Amery; Messrs Heinemann from *Winston Churchill* by Mr Randolph Churchill; and the Controller of H.M. Stationery Office, from Crown Copyright material held in the Public Record Office.

I received much kindness and cooperation from Captain Stephen Roskill and from my colleagues Professors Max Beloff and Norman Gibbs. But my thanks are above all due to the graduate students whom I have taught and examined over the last fifteen years; not only for the information which I have pillaged from their theses (all too many of which are still unpublished) but for the continued stimulus they have provided in discussion of the subject matter of these lectures. In particular Dr Howard Moon, Dr Neil Summerton, Dr Paul Guinn and Mr John Lippincott have taught me far more about various aspects of British defence policy than they can ever have learned from me. It is to them and to their colleagues in the Universities of London and Oxford that this volume is gratefully dedicated.

Oxford, March 1972 MICHAEL HOWARD

1 The Defence of Empire, 1900–1907

The student of contemporary defence policy who tries to educate his judgment by studying the manner in which that policy has developed since the beginning of this century will find himself, throughout his journey, traversing very familiar ground.

Seventy years is a short span in the history of a nation, and although during that time much may have changed in our society, at least our geographical location has not. The British Isles still lie adjacent, but not contiguous, to a European continent peopled by nations whose culture has no more in common with our own than has that of countries founded by men of our own stock in such inconveniently distant parts of the world as North America, the Antipodes and even Southern Africa. Our trading system still runs in channels established over centuries by merchant adventurers in the Indian Ocean, the Pacific and the Caribbean, in the wake of whose activities a political, military and cultural community developed which cannot, even if it should, be very easily dissolved. And we still, at the moment of writing, retain institutional habits and practical interests which tie down units of our armed forces at the other end of the world. Yet basically our security remains involved with that of our continental neighbours: for the dominance of the European land-mass by an alien and hostile power would make almost impossible the maintenance of our national independence, to say nothing of our capacity to maintain a defensive system to protect any extra-European interests we may retain.

The division of our attention between Europe and the rest of the world; the degree of commitment to and involvement in the politics of Europe; the obligations we retain to the dependent but distant states for whose security we are or were at one time responsible; the apportionment of resources between expensive armed forces; above all, the identification and assessment of military threats, and the judgment as to how much of national resources can be spared to deal with them: all this still remains the stuff of British defence policy, as it did at the beginning of the century.

Yet, great as the continuity of concern may be, Britain's Imperial past now seems to most of us very remote indeed. The Diamond Jubilee of Queen Victoria, with its Imperial contingents marching in glittering procession through the streets of London, fresh as it is in the memory of some of our parents, must seem to our children as distant as the barbaric triumphs of ancient Rome. From those dazzling heights of Empire the descent to our present position in the world-scene may appear vertiginous. It was not of Imperial power that British statesmen were primarily conscious at the beginning of this century. They were far more conscious of Imperial weakness: of commitments all over the world to be defended, of well-armed and rapacious adversaries who threatened them, and of very slender resources to protect them with. Pride may well have filled the hearts of those who watched the Jubilee procession, but to those responsible for its safety the Empire appeared rather in the image coined a little later by Sir Thomas Sanderson, then the Permanent Under-Secretary at the Foreign Office, who wrote it has sometimes seemed to me that to a foreigner reading our press the British Empire must appear in the light of some huge giant sprawling over the globe, with gouty fingers and toes stretched in every direction, which cannot be approached without eliciting a scream.[1]

Jan Christian Smuts, the young Transvaal lawyer who within a few months was to be fighting the giant, had already quite correctly diagnosed the Empire as 'a ram-shackle structure,' dominating

great countries largely inhabited by antagonistic peoples, without any adequate military organization designed to keep the peace in case of disturbance or attack. The dominion that the British Empire exercises over the many tribes and peoples within its jurisdiction rests more upon prestige and moral intimidation than upon true military strength.[2]

And within three years Joseph Chamberlain, at the Imperial Conference of 1902, was to speak pathetically of the Empire as a 'weary Titan staggering under the too vast orb of his own fate,' and was without very much success to urge the white colonies to come to their parent's help.[3]

The importance of the Boer War in exposing the underlying weakness of the imperial structure has been quite properly stressed by every historian who has dealt with it. In many ways it was a classic war of Imperial expansion. It was waged, like so many in India, against a tribe whose independence and agitation beyond the Imperial frontier threatened Imperial authority within it; a tribe, like those in the Sudan a few years earlier, to be chastised for insolence, subjugated, civilized, and converted into yet another docile partner in the great Imperial Mission of which Cecil Rhodes, Alfred Milner and the growing band of their disciples were so understandably proud. Nor was its course very different from earlier Imperial wars: the initial disasters, the success once the problems of logistics and tactics were mastered, the prolonged period of pacification, the eventual political settlement. But no previous Imperial war had so drained the Imperial Treasury, had so totally absorbed the available manpower of the British Army, or had subjected its leaders to a test quite so alarmingly similar to that they would have to meet if they ever engaged a European adversary.

All I saw [wrote Leopold Amery of the weeks he passed in South Africa before the outbreak of war] during those weeks left on my mind an ineffaceable impression of the incapacity of many of our senior officers, or the uselessness of most of our then army training for the purposes of modern war especially in South African conditions, and of the urgent need of complete, revolutionary reform of the Army from top to bottom.[4]

When afterwards Amery settled down to write for *The Times* his *History of the War in South Africa*, he did so quite frankly as propaganda for army reform. 'It was only to be effective as a propagandist,' he wrote, 'that I found myself forced to be a serious military historian.'[5] This motive led him perhaps, as a military historian, to be less than fair to the British Army; to give rather too much emphasis to the disasters of Black Week and too little to the strategic and logistical skill which took Lord Roberts to Pretoria within six months of his landing in Cape Town. And seventy years' further experience of insurgency and counter-insurgency warfare may lead us to wonder, not that Lord Kitchener's subsequent pacification campaign took so long and involved some incidental brutalities, but that it did not take still longer and involve yet more. Nevertheless, when the Peace of Vereeniging was signed in 1902, certain disagreeable truths were evident and required emphasis. The British Empire was isolated, not particularly splendidly, in a world of highly armed states, with a Navy whose supremacy still depended on the divisions among her adversaries and an Army incapable of taking the field against any single one of them.

This was the situation which confronted the Committee of Imperial Defence when Balfour assembled it for the first time in 1902 to consider the problems of the British Empire as a whole. Of the numerous problems, including the defence of ports, dockyards, coaling stations, fortresses and occupied territories, which confronted them, two stood out as being of pre-eminent importance. The first was the defence of the United Kingdom itself against a possible invasion from the Continent—in particular, at that time, by France. The second was the defence of India against a possible invasion by Russia. Subsidiary to these was the defence of Britain's route to India through the Mediterranean against a naval combination of both adversaries; which meant, since the virtual abandonment of the decaying Ottoman Empire during the previous decade, primarily the defence of Egypt. Home Defence, Mediterranean and Middle East, Far East: three interlocking problems which perplex us still. And beyond India, the white colonies of the Antipodes were disturbed by the growth of Japanese power even if the British, who saw in it a convenient counterpoise to the Russians, were not. As for the Western Hemisphere, British defence responsibilities comprised, in defiance of the Monroe Doctrine, not only the huge territory of Canada but substantial possessions in the Caribbean and Central America as well. How were these to fare in the face of a United States beginning to wake up to its Manifest Destiny?

Of all these dangers, that which loomed largest in 1902

was the expansion of the Russian Empire. The menace of France had dwindled greatly since the successful confrontation over Fashoda four years earlier; and the French Navy itself under the incompetent administration of M. Pelletan, was falling on evil days.[6] But the Russian fleet was growing alarmingly with the construction authorized under the 1898 programme;[7] and perhaps even more dangerous, and far less easy to counter, the Russian threat to India was growing just as alarmingly with the development of the railway system in Central Russia.[8]

India was at once the most splendid and the most vulnerable of Britain's possessions. 'A quarrel with Russia anywhere, about anything, means the invasion of India,' Balfour reminded his Foreign Secretary, Lord Lansdowne, in 1901.[9] The Viceroy Lord Curzon showed the zeal of the missionary when he wrote in the same year 'As long as we rule India we are the greatest power in the world. If we lose it we shall drop straight away to a third rate power.'[10] It was with the insight of the prophet he wrote seven years later that, once British rule in India was ended, then 'Your ports and your coaling stations, your fortresses and dockyards, your Crown Colonies and protectorates will go too. For either they will be unnecessary, as the toll-gates and barbicans of an Empire that has vanished, or they will be taken by an enemy more powerful than yourselves.'[11]

For Curzon, as for many others, India was what the British Empire was all about. The route to India throughout its length from the Levant to Baluchistan was flanked by Russian power. Russia and Britain competed for influence in 'the Great Game' throughout the Ottoman Empire, Persia and Afghanistan, and had been doing so for fifty years past. This competition shaped the political consciousness of a generation. Curzon himself had won pristine laurels debating at Eton in 1877 about the dangers of the Russian approach to India.[12] Ten years later, the 14-year-old Leopold Amery, when asked on arriving at Harrow School what was the most important event that had taken place in the summer holidays replied precociously: 'The Nizam of Hyderabad's offer to the Queen to supply money and troops in case of trouble with Russia.'[13] Curzon also saw in this offer the first symptom of the transformation of India from a dependency to be held down to an active partner in Imperial defence. 'Not a war can take place in any part of the British Empire,' he boasted in 1909, 'in which Indian princes do not come forward with voluntary offers of armed assistance.'[14] But his pride reflected a more deeply felt and widespread fear that Russian power threatened, not only the road to India, but British rule in India itself: that under serious pressure from outside, the charisma which enabled the British to rule India, the 'moral intimidation' of which Smuts had written, would lose its magic.

Sir Charles Dilke and Spenser Wilkinson, the leading British military writers of the late Victorian age, expressed this fear in the influential study *Imperial Defence* published in 1892, of which they devoted more than a quarter to the geography and politics of the North West Frontier. British rule in India, they pointed out rested, not on force but on self-confidence, which

has produced in [the Indians] a corresponding belief in the omnipotence of Great Britain. . . . Any weakening of this confidence in the minds of the English or of the Indians would be dangerous, and it seems certain that this is one of the difficulties of the present situation. The report has gone forth in India that there is another race, the Russian, which faces British audacity with an audacity of its own.[15]

And, they might have added, a new and sinister portent had appeared only seven years before, with the foundation of the Indian National Congress in 1885. The British were to need in India, in the coming century, all the charisma they could get; and the need to maintain it was a factor which British military planners during the next fifty years seldom allowed their political masters to forget.

How self-confident were the British themselves? In 1909 we find Curzon, returned from his Viceroyalty, urging the young to go forth and man the ramparts of Empire on those distant frontiers which were, he declared with true Curzonian hyperbole 'as essential to the defence of the Empire as the defence of the Channel itself.'[16] In a famous Romanes Lecture at Oxford he sang the praises of those frontiers 'where the machine is relatively impotent and the individual is strong, [and where] is to be found an ennobling and invigorating stimulus for our youth, saving them alike from the corroding ease and the morbid excitements of Western Civilization. . . . Let the advance guard of Empire,' he said 'march forth! The frontiers of Empire continue to beckon.'[17] And out they went, as Newbolt's poem reminds us, from schools specifically designed to fit them for such service, to their frontier graves far away.[18] But if there was to be a serious trouble with the Russians, the defence of India would call for more than a handful of young Oxonians who could be relied on, as District Officers or Army subalterns, to keep the tribes in order. Britain might have the ships, but did she have the men? Above all, did she have the money?

Of the eighty-odd meetings of the Committee of Imperial Defence held between 1902 and 1905 under the Chairmanship of Mr Balfour, the defence of India was discussed at more than fifty, and often it occupied the entire proceedings. As to who should pay for that defence, an unending bureaucratic battle grumbled on between London and Delhi until the eve of the Second World War. 'It is,' Lord Selborne reminded the Viceroy in January 1903, 'a terrific task to remain the greatest naval power when naval powers are year by year increasing in numbers and in strength and at the same time be a military power strong enough to meet the greatest military Power in Asia.'[19] A year later Balfour suggested that 'were India successfully invaded, the moral loss would be incalculable, the material loss would be important—but the burden of British taxation would undergo a most notable diminution!'[20] Even Russia's defeat in the Russo-Japanese War was converted into an evil omen by Lord Esher, that most influential of all advisers on defence questions. 'A similar series of disasters to us,' he noted in March 1905

> would destroy the Empire, as although we might not have a street revolution, we should inevitably have an overwhelming party in favour of reducing the sacrifice in blood and money on the altar of Imperial rule. It would be a case of 'India is not worth a shilling on the Income Tax, or the lives of 50,000 street-bred people.'[21]

From this view the Liberal Government which came into power at the end of that year would have found it hard to dissent.

Of course Indian defence was far from being a one-way traffic. As Professor Thornton reminded us in his indispensable study, *The Imperial Idea and Its Enemies*,[22] Indian troops had been used in the Crimea in 1854–6, in Persia in 1856–7, in China in 1859, in New Zealand in 1860–1, in Abyssinia in 1867, in Malaya in 1875, in Malta in 1878, in Afghanistan from 1878–81, in Egypt in 1882, in the Sudan in 1885, in Suakin garrison until 1895, in Mombasa in 1896, and in the Sudan again from 1896 until 1899. Lord Salisbury referred to—and did not himself resist—the temptation to regard India as 'an English barrack in the Oriental Seas from which we may draw any number of troops without paying for them.'[23] The use of such forces beyond the confines of India had, it is true, required Parliamentary sanction ever since 1858; yet as Sir Charles Lucas, the official historian of India's contribution to the First World War, has emphasized, 'Almost every expedition beyond the confines of India in which troops, whether white or coloured, borne upon the Indian establishment, were employed, led to friction between the Indian and the Home Governments;'[24] and to this the greatest such expedition of all, the campaign in Mesopotamia, during the First World War was to be no exception.

There was no less friction over the defence of India itself. There were nearly 75,000 British troops in India, and had been since the mutiny; together with an Indian Army 150,000 strong.[25] It had long been accepted by the Army in India that India should be defended, not on Indian soil, but in Afghanistan; and that Russian invasion across the Oxus should be countered by an immediate advance on Kabul. For this the Commander in Chief, Sir Frederick Roberts, had estimated in 1892 that he would need 30,000 men from the United Kingdom as first-line reinforcements. When he was informed from London that he must plan on the assumption that no such reinforcements would be forthcoming he replied that if the Indian government was thrown on its own resources it would be reduced to bankruptcy.[26] Eight years later Curzon put forward the same figures: 30,000 men immediately, 70,000 if the war was prolonged. With the War Office at its wits end to find men for South Africa it is hardly surprising that he had no better success. But the first serious examination in London of the basic requirements for

Indian defence, carried out in 1901 and presented to the Committee of Imperial Defence the following year, came to the same conclusion: 30,000 men would be needed at once, and two Army Corps, 70,000 men in all, should be made available on the outbreak of war.[27]

Yet by 1904 even this figure looked too low. Kitchener had now gone out as Commander in Chief with the purpose of organizing the Indian Army for large-scale warfare instead of the frontier skirmishing and internal security duties which had previously occupied it. The Russians had completed their railway from Orenburg to Tashkent which would, it was thought, enable them to pour troops by the hundred thousand over the Oxus. By the end of the year the Committee of Imperial Defence was considering demands from Delhi for nearly 160,000 men; which if met, it was pointed out, would leave in the United Kingdom only 6 cavalry regiments, 79 partly-manned artillery batteries and 15 infantry battalions 'without any rank and file.'[28] And for Kitchener this requirement was only the beginning. In the second year of the war, he claimed, India might need another 300,000–400,000 men; though to maintain such a force in the Hindu Kush, fifteen marches from a railhead, would require, according to the calculations of the Secretary of the Committee of Imperial Defence, Sir George Clarke, no less than three million camels.[29] The Sub-Committee of the Committee of Imperial Defence under Lord Morley which the Liberal Government set up in 1907 to examine the whole question came back to the figure of 100,000 men, laying it down that 'a military organization at home that would enable 100,000 men to be sent to India in the first year of a war, appears a military necessity.' As for Kitchener's further estimates—which Lord Roberts as an expert witness, increased to 500,000—the Committee did not commit themselves; but 'whatever the figures may be', they recorded,

> that a war with Russia for preponderating influence in
> Afghanistan and ultimately for dominion in India would
> entail immense demands and vast sacrifices, is beyond all
> doubt.[30]

This, then, was the main task that confronted the British
Army. India, in the view of the Committee of Imperial
Defence, of Parliament and of the British public, was the
destination of the Expeditionary Force which the War
Office was organizing in 1906–7, even if the General Staff
already had another role in mind for it.[31] For on one issue at
least, the British Government had at last made up its mind.
The British Army need not be tied down to the protection
of the British Isles.

It is easy to ignore, or to discount as a historical curiosity,
the decennial invasion scares which swept the British Isles
during the nineteenth century. Yet it was not self-evident
that the insular invulnerability on which British policy had
depended for so long could survive each new wave of technological change which that century witnessed. The advent of
steam in the 1840s; of ironclads in the 1860s; of German
organization for rapid mobilization in the 1870s; of technical
feasibility of a Channel Tunnel in the 1880s: each had led,
very properly, to a reexamination of the basic assumptions
on which British defence policy rested. If in 1900 there was
no technological innovation to alarm the British public, the
political situation more than made up for it. Britain had not a
friend in Europe; the French and German press, if not their
Governments, were quite explicit in their enmity; and the
entire Regular Army was out of the country. The popular
Press was in a state of wild alarm. In Black Week 1899,
W. T. Stead, writing in *The Review of Reviews*, suggested

that 'passionate determination to hoist the Union Jack over Pretoria may result in our seeing next year the Tricolour flying—temporarily at least—over the Palace at Westminster.' A few months later he suggested that all the German waiters in London, armed with cudgels and revolvers, would converge on Woolwich and seize the Arsenal. Official opinion was only slightly less alarmed. In February 1900 the Under-Secretary of State for War called for 120,000 volunteers to guard the country against hostile raids. In May the Prime Minister himself, the usually phlegmatic Lord Salisbury, warning that all the developing powers of offence on the Continent might 'be united in one great wave to dash upon our shores,' called for the establishment of a network of rifle clubs throughout the country. And the Commander in Chief, Lord Wolseley, advised confidentially that unless three new Army Corps were made available for Home Defence, 'the protection of these islands will depend solely and entirely on the Fleet.'[32]

An influential and vociferous school of thought, which included, not surprisingly, most of the senior officers in the Royal Navy, saw nothing wrong with that. The 'Blue Water' controversy over the role of the Navy was already nearly twenty years old, and it was not to be resolved until, twenty years later, the advent of air power lifted it on to a new level. But in 1903 Balfour had the Committee of Imperial Defence examine the whole question of Britain's vulnerability to invasion, and this examination reached conclusions that satisfied him and most of his colleagues; though not, as we shall see later, a substantial section of the British public led by *The Times* Military Correspondent, Colonel Repington, by Lord Roberts and by that powerful pressure-group, the National Service League.

The protection of the United Kingdom, the Committee

of Imperial Defence now concluded, did indeed depend on
the Fleet. If the Fleet did fail to protect them no invasion
would be needed: Britain would simply starve. The Fleet
might not be able to prevent small detachments of enemy
troops getting across the sea, but these could be dealt with
by the Militia and the Volunteers. The Army should therefore be organized primarily for its overseas role.[33] 'The
investigation,' reported Balfour in November 1903, 'seems
to me to point unmistakably to the conclusion that the
chief military problem which this country has to face is that
of Indian, rather than Home Defence.'[34] This view was
endorsed by Lord Esher when, early in 1905, he drew up a
statement of principles on which the new Army was to be
based. 'It is *not*,' he insisted, 'to be organized for the defence of these shores, but is intended to take the field, at any
threatened point where the interests of the Empire are im-
perilled, and especially on the North-West Frontier of
India.'[35]

So much for the two great staples of Empire, the British
Isles themselves and the Indian sub-continent. As for the
rest—the colonies, the dependencies, the bases, the coaling
stations—fundamentally the Navy defended these as well;
though 'defence' in this context was a rather deceptive term.
Long before Captain Mahan had enunciated in the United
States that doctrine of 'Command of the Sea' which sank so
rapidly into naval heads, there to ossify into impenetrable
orthodoxy, the British writer Sir John Colomb had traced
the connection between naval supremacy and imperial defence. His work on *The Protection of Commerce and the
Distribution of our War Forces* had been published as early
as 1867. *The Cambridge History of the British Empire*
described it as 'the first satisfactory and comprehensive

statement of the problems of Imperial Defence'; the Australian press, less easily impressed, called Colomb 'a fussy busybody'.[36] For Colomb insisted that the function of the Navy was not to scatter itself in the local defensive roles that the colonies naturally demanded, but to blockade the enemy's ports and defeat his main forces, thus freeing from enemy threat the sea routes which linked the naval and commercial bases of the Empire. The Navy, he insisted, protected the Empire by maintaining the offensive: taking the war to the enemy's coasts and keeping it there.

By the end of the nineteenth century this view had become quite explicitly the basis of the Royal Navy's strategic doctrine. It was laid down in a much-quoted document which the Colonial Defence Committee printed in 1896 for the instruction of officials throughout the Empire responsible for defence questions:

> The maintenance of sea supremacy [this ran] has been assumed as the basis of the system of Imperial Defence against attack over the sea. This is the determining factor in shaping the whole defensive policy of the Empire, and is fully recognized by the Admiralty, who have accepted the responsibility of protecting all British territory abroad against organized invasion from the sea. To fulfil this charge, they claim the absolute power of disposing of their forces in the manner they consider most certain to secure success, and object to limit [*sic*] the action of any part of them to the immediate neighbourhood of places which they consider may be more effectively protected by operations at a distance.[37]

This was lucid, logical and authoritative; but the authority was one which the colonies remained very reluctant indeed to accept.

It was in 1887 that delegates from the colonies had assembled in London for the first time to talk about the problems of their common defence. That they *had* a common problem was something of which they were only intermittently aware. For some thirty years past they had indeed contributed forces to Britain's military campaigns. It had perhaps been mainly a combination of cousinly sympathy with a desire not to be left out of any adventures that were going that had inspired the very remarkable colonial interest in the Crimean War. For the purposes of that war they contributed £143,000 to a Patriotic Fund, and a body of Canadian volunteers actually fought; a portent as significant, in its way, as the presence of the contingent from the Kingdom of Sardinia. But by 1877 they had more immediate reasons to worry. Russia was a naval power not to be taken lightly. Both in Australia and in Canada anxious discussions took place as to how to fend off possible raids on their coasts by predatory Russian squadrons if the Balkan crisis erupted into hostilities. The Australians considered buying an ironclad of their own. The Canadians, having assessed the cost of fortifying their coasts, considered whether it might not be cheaper to allow the Russians to destroy everything within reach of their guns and then build it again afterwards.[38] The crisis blew over, but the lesson was clear: British citizens might emigrate to the uttermost parts of the earth, but so long as they remained within the British Empire it would be difficult to escape involvement in Britain's wars. For many of them the lesson was equally clear, that since such wars were the responsibility of British statesmen in London, London should bear the cost of preparing for them.

The Commission which was set up under the Earl of Carnarvon in 1879 to study the problems of Imperial Defence could 'see no reason why the Australian Colonies should not make a moderate contribution in money towards the cost of [naval forces] . . . maintained by the mother country for the protection of interests common to the Colonies and herself.' But they admitted that it was 'not yet possible to define with accuracy the conditions upon which to determine the relative apportionment of the burdens as between the mother country and her colonies.'[39] It was to remain impossible for many years to come.

At the 1887 Conference a kind of 'pilot project' was set up for cooperation in the field of Imperial Defence. After long and hard bargaining it was agreed that the Royal Navy should establish an Auxiliary Squadron in Australian waters. The Australian colonies were to pay £126,000 a year towards the cost of its upkeep. Its command was to be in the hands of the British Commander-in-Chief of the Australian station, but its ships were not to be moved from Australian waters without the consent of the colonial governments concerned.[40] If this arrangement had worked it might have provided a model for similar arrangements throughout the Empire. In fact it resulted only in continuing bitterness and friction. The Australian press denounced what they called 'naval tribute'. Australian politicians objected to anything resembling a subsidy to the government in London. The Admiralty for its part made very clear their dislike of having forces tied down which in their opinion could be better employed elsewhere, and they accepted the arrangement with the worst possible grace. Their attempts to reverse it succeeded in 1903, when the Australian government abandoned its veto on the movement of ships and agreed to pay (with New Zealand) half the cost of a squadron to be stationed in Eastern waters. But this new arrangement, by which the Australian tax-payer paid for ships which he seldom saw and over which he had no control, proved even less acceptable than the old.[41] The scheme was revised in 1909 to take account of Australian objections, but in 1914 Australians were still complaining about the vulnerability of their coasts to enemy attack.

The whole question of Imperial Defence, indeed, presented during this period a succession of almost insoluble political problems, and the series of Imperial Conferences which were held between 1897 and 1911 did little more than bring existing differences into the open. The British government, inevitably, saw the problem as one of eliciting from each part of the Empire contributions to the defence of the whole—contributions to be used according to a strategy worked out by a central authority. The colonies, isolated from Britain and from one another, were concerned with getting the maximum reassurances about contributions to their own defence; and the idea of any central authority, however powerful their own representation on it, was one which, with the exception only of New Zealand, they were temperamentally inclined to regard with profound suspicion. When in 1902 Joseph Chamberlain brought forward his proposal for 'A Common Council of Empire', the idea had a chilling reception, and it fared no better when the Liberals revived it five years later. Sir Wilfred Laurier of Canada voiced the principal objections. First, the colonies resented the creation of any body based on London which might override the autonomy of their own legislatures. Secondly they did not desire any responsibilities which might involve them in Continental politics, tainted as these were with the militarism identified by Laurier as 'the curse and blight of Europe'. Had the assembled delegates at the pre-war Imperial Conferences been able to foresee that by the end of the next decade the representatives of Canada, Australia and South Africa would be presiding over committees to redraw European boundaries after a European war in which the British Empire had lost a million dead, they would have been unlikely to reconsider their attitude. The most that could be achieved, in 1907, was agreement to set up that process of institutionalized and regular consultation which has continued in the shape of Commonwealth Prime Ministers' Conferences, to our own day; together with a rather ill-defined right of attendance by Dominion representatives at the Committee of Imperial Defence when questions relevant to their interests were being discussed.[42]

The British Government might therefore have been forgiven if it regarded the colonies as liabilities rather than assets on the balance sheet of Imperial Defence, consuming much security and producing little, if it had not been for the contribution which they had made to the South African War. Here there was no question of their own security being involved. No Boer gunboats were likely to threaten Sydney or Vancouver. Yet in response to popular demand the Canadian, Australian and New Zealand Governments sent contingents of volunteers to South Africa, to fight for what was, for them, a purely ideological issue. These contingents were small, but they were deeply symbolic.[43] Imperial organization might be rudimentary and Imperial strategy non-existent, but there was no question of the strength of Imperial sentiment. There was little doubt that if Britain did become involved in another major war, volunteers would come from the colonies to help her as fast as boats could bring them.

By the end of the decade it was clear that these volunteers would be more than unorganized and untrained enthusiasts. The approach, of the British War Office to the problem of Imperial Defence, especially during Haldane's tenure of office as Secretary of State for War, was significantly different from that of the Admiralty. At the Imperial

Conference of 1907 the Admiralty maintained, in the face of all colonial objections, their insistence on unified command of all Imperial Fleets. The War Office on the other hand simply submitted memoranda drawing attention to the military advantages to be gained by uniformity in organization, staff procedure, training and equipment, and discreetly offering the services of the General Staff—which might one day, they hinted, become a true Imperial Staff, drawing its members from throughout the Empire—to assist the colonies in any way they desired. These documents were received with unanimous approval by the Conference, which sanctioned the development of such an Imperial Staff to 'advise as to the training, education and war organization of the military forces of the Crown in every part of the Empire.'[44] Two years later, at the Conference on the Naval and Military Needs of the Empire of 1909, more precise measures were agreed to standardize the military organization and equipment of what were now the self-governing Dominions along British lines, so that, as Asquith explained to the House of Commons, 'while the Dominion troops would in each case be raised for the defence of the Dominion concerned, it would be made readily practicable in case of need for that Dominion to mobilize and use them for the defence of the Empire as a whole.'[45] Thanks to these agreements, by 1914 a very considerable degree of uniformity of organization, equipment and doctrine had actually come to exist among the armed forces of the British Empire.

The contribution which the Dominions could make to the defence of the Empire was thus far from negligible, but it was at best limited, and always quite incalculable. Whatever they did, the burdens of Imperial Defence would still rest overwhelmingly on the shoulders of the Royal Navy. But the

Navy could do nothing to defend India. That would require an Army and one, as we have seen, of quite horrifying size. The Navy could do equally little to defend Canada. As the First Lord of the Admiralty, Lord Selborne, observed in April 1901, 'If the Americans choose to pay for what they can easily afford, they can build up a navy fully as large and then larger than ours, and I am not sure they will not do it.'[46] And with the growth of German and Japanese as well as the Russian and the French fleets, it was even doubtful whether the Navy could command the seas against the most likely combination of its European adversaries. A building programme such as the Navy League urged, to guarantee 'command of the sea against all comers' would involve public expenditure on a scale which the Balfour Administration regarded as inconceivable. Only diplomacy could solve the strategists' dilemma.

This was not to be the last time in the twentieth century that a British government, faced with a possible combination of enemies to arm against which has involved sacrifices on a scale it dared not demand from its electorate, tried to escape from its predicament by a policy of 'appeasement'. Its success in the five years between 1902 and 1907 enabled Britain to wage a war which brought her to the peak of her Imperial power. Its failure in the five years between 1934 and 1939 resulted in a conflict which led to the disintegration of her Empire and which might, but for the mistakes of her adversaries, have resulted in her own subjugation to an alien and very much less tolerable imperial rule. As it was, British diplomacy between 1902 and 1907 was able to reduce the task of British military planners to a manageable size. There was the tacit decision not under any circumstances to become involved in armed conflict with the United States— tacit, yet made quite explicit by the abandonment of the bases at Halifax and Esquimault, the closing of the Jamaica dockyards and the abolition of the West Indian and North American squadrons. There was, in 1902, the Anglo-Japanese Alliance, which enabled the Royal Navy to concentrate on the task of matching Franco-Russian strength in European waters. Two years later came the business-like settlement of colonial differences with France; and finally in 1907, over the bewildered objections of the Government of India, came the *détente* with Russia. It added up to a quite remarkable feat of diplomatic pacification. In 1901 the British Empire had stood alone in unpopular isolation. By 1908 she was on increasingly friendly terms both with her traditional imperial rivals, France and Russia, and with the new naval powers on the other side of the world, the United States and Japan. But neither the Royal Navy nor the General Staff felt in the least *désoeuvré* by this transformation of the international scene. For some time past, their sights had been set on a yet more formidable foe.

2 The Balance of Power, 1905–1914

The origins of the tension which developed between Great
Britain and Germany at the end of the nineteenth century
have been exhaustively described and analysed, and one
thing at least can be said of them with little fear of contra-
diction. They cannot be attributed to simple political or
commercial rivalries. On both sides popular emotion ran
faster and further than government policy. A careful calculation of state interests on both sides might have led, not
perhaps to alliance, but at least to a *détente* comparable to
that which British diplomats negotiated so successfully with
France and Russia. The fundamental requirements for such
a *détente* would have been on the one hand, British abstention from involvement in the Continental military balance
which Germany saw as vital to her own security, and, on the
other, German abstention from challenging the naval pre-
eminence on which the British believed that their survival
and that of the entire imperial system depended.

In Britain both popular and official opinion did in fact
remain deeply hostile to the whole concept of any military
involvement on the Continent; so hostile, indeed, that it
was not evident to anyone until war had actually broken out
whether a British Expeditionary Force would be committed
there or not. In Germany on the other hand the new naval
policy reflected deep currents of popular emotion and

powerful economic interests which were concerned with a great deal more than national security.[47] The status as a World Power (*Weltmacht*) to which the Second Reich aspired may have been a more moderate and indeed a more legitimate ambition than the World Domination (*Weltherrschaft*) which, many scholars now agree, was the ultimate aim of the Third Reich.[48] World Imperial status for Germany was something to which, as such, the British government had no objection. The Berlin–Baghdad railway was approved by the British Government, over the protests of British financial interests. The development of a German colonial system was rather favoured than otherwise in London—if only because, as Winston Churchill told the Committee of Imperial Defence in July, 1912 'we should be rather glad to see what is now concentrated dissipated.'[49] It was indeed precisely the failure of German power to find an outlet and its consequent concentration in Europe, its lack of any significant possessions overseas, that made it so peculiarly menacing to the sprawling British Empire in two World Wars, and which make so misleading all arguments about 'traditional' British strategy drawn from earlier conflicts against the Spanish and French Empires, with all the colonial hostages they had offered to fortune and the Royal Navy. But the German interests pressing for the development of world power were not concerned with expanding within what they saw as a British dominated world-system. It was precisely that system which they found intolerable, and which they were determined to challenge on a basis of equality. This required rather more in the way of battleships than the *Risikoflotte* with which Tirpitz introduced the Reichstag at the end of 1899 to the tempting, but expensive, prospect of naval might.

The Royal Navy appreciated the significance of the challenge as early as 1902. Lord Selborne, as First Lord of the Admiralty, explained to the Cabinet in October of that year how the design of the new German battle fleet made it clear that it was intended as a fighting force for the North Sea only. The powerful naval lobby in England loudly demanded appropriate steps to meet the challenge.[50] But the diplomatic documents do not suggest that this was a serious factor in the Anglo–French agreements of 1904. For the Committee of Imperial Defence Russia remained the principal adversary against whom preparation had to be made at least until 1907.[51] But in the *détente* which was negotiated with Russia in that year, fear of Germany played a quite palpable role. We are now considerably better informed about the part which such Foreign Office officials as Sir Francis Bertie, Sir Louis Mallet, Sir Charles Hardinge and Sir Eyre Crowe were beginning to play in the formulation of British policy; about the clarity with which they perceived the threat posed by German ambitions, not so much to British world interests as to the European balance of power with which they were professionally concerned; and about the degree of influence they were able to exercise over Sir Edward Grey.[52] British rejoicing at Russia's defeat at the hands of the Japanese in 1904–5 was short lived. The Admiralty, which for so many decades had used the size of the Russian fleet as a standard for their own building programme, now saw in its destruction at Tsushima a compelling reason for laying down yet more keels against Germany. The General Staff in 1906 urged the need to reconstitute Russian power as a makeweight to Germany in Europe; and Grey himself, within a few days of coming into office, wrote in February 1906 that he was 'impatient to see Russia reestablished as a factor in European politics.'[53] It was ironic that the party which traditionally regarded the whole concept of 'the balance of power' with such profound suspicion should assume office almost at the exact moment when, for the first time for nearly a century, that concept was assuming so inescapable a relevance to the security of their country.

The idea of the Balance of Power was not only alien to liberal and radical thought. It was alien to Imperial thought as well. Leo Amery, the most vigorous of the young Edwardian Imperialists, was to suggest to Lord Milner in 1915 that 'the war against a German domination in Europe was only necessary because we had failed to make ourselves sufficiently strong and united to be able to afford to disregard the European balance.'[54] Two years later Lord Milner expressed to General Sir Henry Wilson the 'vague hope that, in future, we might be able to keep out of European complications, saying that the Dominions have vast potentialities and that if we link up closely we would be strong enough to defy all comers.'[55] This view, that the Empire would enable Britain to stand aloof from Europe, that it might indeed provide an alternative to Europe, was to remain influential with Milner's disciples of the *Round Table* who were to be, between the wars, themselves influential men. Naval thinkers naturally sympathized with it; the command of the seas was intended to replace rather than to supplement the balance of power. But what about the Army?

The preservation of the Balance of Power in Europe had been one of the justifications for the maintenance of armed forces in peacetime given in the preamble to the Annual Mutiny Act until 1868. Then, two years after the Prussian Army had transformed the Balance of Power at the Battle of Königgrätz, a member of the House of Commons suggested that such a claim was patently ridiculous, and it was quietly dropped.[56] The Army did not lose sight completely in its thinking of the possible requirements of European warfare. The 'Stanhope Memorandum' of 1888 listed continental intervention as a possible role for the British Army, although giving it the lowest of priorities.[57] But in 1901, in the magisterial survey of 'the Military Needs of the Empire in a War with France and Russia' with which the C.I.D. 'A' Series of papers begins, Lt. Col. E. A. Altham proposed a revised organization for the Army which would, he suggested, not only

> supply for the Empire an effective force ... [but] give an appreciable value to our alliance in war, not merely as that of a great naval power, but also as that of an ally which, by virtue of its sea command, could choose its own point to strike at, and then throw into the scales at short notice an effective army of about 200,000 men. Even by Germany aid of this description could not be despised, and would tend to make it more reasonable that she should support Great Britain in a war with Russia and France.[58]

Not all Colonel Altham's colleagues at the War Office shared his desire to see the British Army used as a lure for a German alliance. 'Instead of regarding Germany as a possible ally,' Colonel William Robertson argued the following year, 'we should recognize her as our most persistent, deliberate and formidable rival.'[59] But the reemergence of this notion, that a military contribution might make Britain *bündnisfähig* to a Continental ally—the equivalent of Tirpitz's *Risikoflotte* on land—is of some historical significance, and it is not the last that we shall hear of it.

It is not surprising that among the most enthusiastic exponents of the doctrine of the Balance of Power were the officers of the newly constituted General Staff at the War Office; one of whose first tasks, as a result of the Tangier crisis in 1905, was to examine the feasibility of British military intervention on the Continent in the event of British involvement in a Franco-German conflict. They had a professional insight into the problem which the French Army would face in the event of a German attack; and if as a result of their calculations they overestimated the contribution that any British force would make to redressing the military balance,[60] they were not far wrong in their assessment of the moral value which would be attached by the French Armed Forces to the presence of British troops, even in small numbers, fighting by their side. Colonel Spencer Ewart, who became Director of Military Operations in 1906, wrote in his diary two years later: 'If our Expeditionary Force is cut down, then "goodbye" to the *Entente Cordiale* with France . . . the only alternative is a selfish isolation which would lead to a combination of all Europe against us under the dictatorship of Germany.'[61] In the summer of the same year, 1908, the General Staff made an *ex cathedra* pronouncement on the subject to the Committee of Imperial Defence. Britain needed an Army, they stated, to 'maintain the traditional policy of upholding the balance of power in Europe. According as the strength and efficiency of our military forces increase or decrease, so does the value of our friendship to any continental nation.'[62] This statement is the more interesting in that only ten days earlier Lord Esher, a man still highly influential in the formulation of British defence policy, had categorically informed the Chancellor of the Exchequer that the Army was maintained 'for the purposes of reinforcing British troops in India and Egypt and for relieving troops wherever they are quartered abroad.'[63]

Before exploring any further this conflict between the exponents of a Continental and those of an Imperial strategy which came to a head in 1908–1909, we must consider another element in the situation. The two statements quoted above were not contributions to a bilateral debate, but responses to the challenge of yet a third view: the old argument, which had been settled by Mr Balfour's Administration to its satisfaction but which was to be advanced again yet more vigorously under his successor, that the Army—or a substantial part of it—should stay at home to defend the threatened shores of the British Isles.

As we have already seen, the Committee of Imperial Defence had reached the conclusion as early as 1903 that the defence of the United Kingdom could be safely entrusted to the power of the Royal Navy in the first place and the activities of voluntary territorial forces in the second. But this decision, which Mr Balfour announced in the House of Commons in 1905,[64] entirely failed to satisfy a large body of opinion, led by such respected experts as Colonel Repington of *The Times* and Spenser Wilkinson, the military correspondent of the *Morning Post*. This movement demanded the creation of an Army based on compulsory service in order to defend the British Isles. It enlisted as its titular leaders the two greatest figures of the South African War, Lord Milner and Lord Roberts; and it received powerful backing from all those whose fears of invasion multiplied as the size of the German Navy increased and the state of Anglo-German relations grew worse. Such well-known works as Erskine Childers's novel *The Riddle of the Sands* (1903), William Le Queux's *The Invasion of 1910* (written in 1906), Du Maurier's melodrama *An Englishman's Home* (1909) are only a tiny fraction of the great mass of horror stories about the invasion of the British Isles by German troops that filled the popular press and the railway bookstalls in the decade before 1914.[65] In November 1908 Lord Roberts pointed out in the House of Lords that there were already 80,000 trained German soldiers in the United Kingdom; and he persuaded the House to pass a motion calling for 'an Army so strong in numbers and efficient in quality that the most formidable foreign nation would hesitate to attempt a landing on these shores.'[66] The following year—1909, the year of the great dreadnought scare—Lord Curzon joined in the call for compulsory national service to guard against an invasion which, if successful, would result in 'the crumbling and collapse of society itself . . . the utter subversion of the old order of things to which we are accustomed;'[67] and in the Commons the Secretary of State for War was asked to comment on the rumour 'that there are, in a cellar within a quarter of a mile of Charing Cross, 50,000 stands of Mauser rifles and $7\frac{1}{2}$ million Mauser cartridges.' The grave calculations of the Committee of Imperial Defence thus took place against a background of xenophobic paranoia which does much to explain the enthusiasm—almost the relief—with which the outbreak of war appears to have been so widely greeted in 1914.

All this emotion was channelled and exploited by the National Service League, which was founded in 1902 and for ten years never relaxed its pressure for the introduction of compulsory service as the basis for Britain's military system. It was an interesting body which still awaits its historian: an amalgamation of many different and conflicting elements. Most of its members no doubt were concerned with National Service purely as a means for making Britain safe from attack; believing that the part-time soldiers of the Militia and the Volunteers would never be adequate either in numbers or in training to meet the highly professional German

Army if it were ever to land. But the movement contained at least two other elements. One consisted of those who, like Milner and his followers, supported national service on the neo-Hegelian grounds that it was as necessary to the moral well-being of the individual as to the security of the State; the principle, as Amery put it, 'that it is the duty of all citizens to be trained in their youth to the use of arms.'[68] The other elements consisted of those who believed—but found it prudent not to express their beliefs too openly—that a war with Germany was increasingly probable; that if it came it would inevitably involve the British Army in continental operations; and that these would require Britain to arm herself on a continental scale.

This was the view held by Roberts himself. 'We must remember,' he told Winston Churchill in 1912, in trying to enlist his support,

> that the victories which have successfully ended the various crises in the history of our country have taken place, not within these shores or on the seas, but beyond them; and the real reason for raising our Citizen Army on a compulsory basis is that we can never obtain from volunteers during peace the time required for a military training that will fit them to back the Expeditionary Force at the decisive point.[69]

More important, the General Staff itself viewed the agitation with sympathy, for the same reason. Arnold-Forster, Haldane's predecessor as Secretary of State for War, expressed in his diary the view that the Army Council 'had been solidly conscriptionist from its earliest days.'[70] In 1910 General Sir Ian Hamilton told Lady Roberts that virtually the whole General Staff favoured 'conscription on the pure Continental basis.'[71] Hamilton himself, like many other regular officers, did not share this view for reasons which might still command sympathy in military circles today. In a memorandum he wrote on *Compulsory Service* in 1910 for Haldane—probably for the publication it at once received—he criticized the idea of a national service army. It would, he argued, be too expensive, and—lacking the professionalism and offensive spirit of the regulars—it would be useless for the tasks of imperial service and overseas offensive expeditions which were the Army's true *raison d'être*.[72] The question of continental involvement he passed over in understandable silence. Any public reference to it by a senior serving officer would have been intolerable to a Government composed so largely of men who still refused even to contemplate the bare possibility.

The Government did not yield to the pressure of the National Service League. A further study by the Committee of Imperial Defence, in 1908, reiterated its former conclusion:

> that so long as our naval supremacy is assured against any reasonably probable combination of powers, invasion is impracticable ... [but] that our Army for Home Defence ought to be sufficient in numbers and organization not only to repel small raids but to compel an enemy who contemplates invasion to come with so substantial a force as will make it impossible for him to evade our fleets.[73]

The size of this force the Committee of Imperial Defence assessed at 70,000 men; to deal with which, they agreed, two divisions of regular troops might be needed in addition to the Territorial Force which Haldane was constructing out of the old Volunteers. But on National Service the Government stood firm. Liberal and probably national opinion, they considered, was hostile to the idea. Its introduction might provoke Germany to a preemptive attack before the balance of man-power swung too heavily against her. The expense would compete with measures of social reform. The Empire could not be garrisoned with a conscript force. Finally in the words of their new Assistant Secretary, Colonel Maurice Hankey, 'if every man had military training the nation would lose its perspective on the vital importance of sea power.'[74] As so often before, radicals and navalists found themselves in a natural alliance against the spectres of militarism, continental strategy and Balance of Power.

The Army was to remain professional, then, and the greater part of it was to remain available for overseas expedition. Where was it to be sent? The Committee of Imperial Defence, in the document quoted above, still—in October 1908 —spoke only of the 100,000 troops which should be kept available for the defence of India. This must have been about the last occasion on which it did. During the same month Mr Asquith set up a Committee of Imperial Defence Sub-Committee on the Military Needs of the Empire, and the conclusions of that Committee, when it reported in July 1909, pointed in a very different direction.

To understand how this came about, we must retrace our steps to the Tangier crisis of 1905, when the diplomacy of Chancellor von Bülow compelled the British Government to visualize for the first time the possibility of common action with France in a war against Germany. In August of that year the Secretary of the Committee of Imperial Defence, Sir George Clarke, suggested to the Prime Minister that the General Staff should be invited to study the implications for Great Britain of a German invasion of Belgium: 'a study of this kind,' he remarked rather sourly 'is just what the General Staff would like, and they might perhaps be able to achieve more success than in dealing with the Indian frontier.'[75]

To the extent that the General Staff had already focussed on the problem, he was perfectly right. In April 1905 they had already played a War Game[76] from which they deduced the principles which lay behind British strategic thinking for the next nine years: that if the Germans attacked France they would sooner or later have to employ an outflanking movement through Belgium; and that logistical difficulties would compel them to keep the movement within the area limited on its western boundary by the course of the river Meuse; and that if British help was to be effective it would have to be prompt. In September Balfour gave them their official assignment to study the military implications of an infringement by Germany of Belgian neutrality. The conclusion they came to was to shape British military planning until the outbreak of war.

> An efficient army of 120,000 troops [wrote Colonel Callwell of the General Staff on 3 October 1905] might just have the effect of preventing important German successes on the Franco-German frontier and of leading up to the situation that Germany, crushed at sea, also felt herself impotent on land. That would almost certainly bring about a speedy and, from the British and French point of view, satisfactory peace.[77]

The Navy meanwhile had formed their own, rather different conclusions, which also were to shape their thinking, if not until the outbreak of war, then certainly until Winston Churchill became First Lord of the Admiralty in 1911. Since Admiral Sir John Fisher, the First Sea Lord, resolutely refused to create a Naval Staff to formulate any war plans, the views of the Navy at the time of the Tangier crisis were expressed by the Commander in Chief of the

Channel Fleet, Admiral Sir Arthur Wilson. These rested on a realistic appreciation of the restricted influence which the Navy could bring to bear in any war against Germany.

> No action by the Navy alone [wrote Wilson on 27 June 1905] can do France any good. It would amount to little more than the capture of a few colonies from Germany which are of no use to her, and the stoppage of direct oversea trade from her own ports; but as she would probably have direct access to the sea through neutral ports . . . this would not greatly affect her general trade . . . the result [he went on] would depend entirely on the military operations on the French frontier, and we should be bound to devote the whole military forces of the country to endeavour to create a diversion on the coast of Germany in France's favour; also, in view of the rapidity with which events moved in the War of 1870, any diversion to be effective must be made at once.[78]

The officers of the General Staff who examined these naval proposals for 'diversions on the coast of Germany' considered them to be so impracticable that they refused to collaborate any further.[79] On the other hand Fisher was equally appalled at the General Staff's preference for direct help to the French. When in December an informal caucus of the Committee of Imperial Defence under Lord Esher approved the plans of the General Staff, authorized them to make contact with the French, and instructed them to work out 'arrangements for the mobilization and transport to the northern French ports of [an expeditionary] force [of 120,000 men] with the utmost completeness,' Fisher withdrew his representative from the discussions, and thenceforward virtually boycotted the Committee for Imperial Defence.[80]

Thereafter the Admiralty and the General Staff worked out their plans for a war with Germany in mutual isolation.

Naval planning was carried out by a committee meeting during 1906–1907 at the Royal Naval College, Greenwich, under conditions of considerable secrecy, with Captain Hankey of the Royal Marines as its secretary and the naval historian Julian Corbett assisting with general advice. The first part of their report, indeed, was little more than a summary of the ideas which Corbett was to set out in his *Principles of Maritime Strategy* a few years later.[81] In general, the recommendations of this committee were of limited value, since they entirely ignored the possibility of a German attack on France as a *casus belli*. They dealt only with the considerably less likely eventualities of an attack on Holland; of an intensification of the *Drang nach Osten* through the absorption of Austria-Hungary into the German Empire on the death of the Emperor Francis Joseph; and of a possible German attempt to establish colonies in Latin America.

The committee assumed as the basis of its recommendations that 'the loss to German commercial interests through the destruction or enforced idleness of German shipping will be so great that popular outcry will put a stop to further operations.' The plans proposed involved a blockade of Germany, the obstruction of the Elbe, the destruction through bombardment of the Baltic ports, and 'a series of large scale raids . . . anywhere from Kiel to Memel, which would keep the whole littoral in a perpetual state of unrest and alarm.' A German invasion of the Low Countries should be dealt with, they recommended, by the occupation of a German or a Dutch island, preferably Borkum, which would compel the German fleet to come out and fight. The destruction of the German Fleet, the committee agreed, would not save the Low Countries from being overrun, but 'the moral effect would be tremendous, and the political effect, when it comes to negotiations for peace, would be of vast importance.' This was the strategy which had been effective against France in the eighteenth century. It was assumed, rather than argued, that it would be equally effective against Germany in the twentieth.

The General Staff for its part increasingly concentrated after 1906 on the problems of a war against Germany, to the gradual exclusion of all other preoccupations. The armament, training and organization of the British Army was shaped accordingly.[82] It has been very widely assumed that the reorientation of the British Army to European warfare and its commitment to cooperation with the French was largely the work of General Sir Henry Wilson during his tenure of the Directorate of Military Operations between 1910 and 1914. The famous meeting of the Committee of Imperial Defence on 23rd August 1911, at which Wilson out-argued his naval colleague, has been considered equally decisive in the creation of a military commitment to France.[83] But of yet greater significance were the conclusions of a sub-committee of the Committee of Imperial Defence which Asquith set up in October 1908 to consider the military needs of the Empire; to which the General Staff made recommendations which were in essentials identical with those presented by Henry Wilson three years later.[84]

In their paper the General Staff advised quite categorically that an Expeditionary Force of four infantry divisions and one cavalry division should be sent to reinforce the left flank of the French Army, landing at French ports and being ready for action by the twentieth day after mobilization. If the Admiralty's proposals for a blockade and coastal raids were accepted, they argued, the French would be defeated in the field before these could take effect. The committee appears to have found this argument convincing. Lord Esher suggested in vain that Britain should limit her liability to her Ally since 'the pressure which can be brought to bear upon Germany by the threat . . . of seizing her mercantile fleet, by the closing of the Elbe and the Baltic in war, by the deadly injury to her commerce, and the fear of raids . . . might be held to be a sufficient fulfilment of our share in the partnership between us and the French nation'; together perhaps with a token force of 12,000 horsemen 'under a daring and sympathetic commander.'[85] Such proposals for limited liability were to find a more appreciative audience thirty years later.

The Committee's final Report, was issued in July 1909. It stated firmly that 'a military *entente* between Great Britain and France can only be of value so long as it rests on the understanding that, in the event of war in which both are involved alike on land and sea, the whole of the available naval and military strength of the two countries will be brought to bear at the decisive point.' The Report recognized that 'the expediency of sending a military force abroad, or of relying on naval means only, is a matter which can only be determined when the occasion arises, by the Government of the day;' but, it went on,

> in view of the possibility of a decision by the Cabinet to use military force, the Committee has examined the plans of the General Staff and are of the opinion that in the initial stages of a war between France and Germany, in which the British Government decided to support France, the plan to which preference is given by the General Staff is a valuable one, and the General Staff should accordingly work out all the necessary details.

The General Staff needed no prompting, and the confidence with which Henry Wilson was able to expound his plans two years later when the Committee of Imperial

Defence met at the height of the Agadir crisis owed more than has been generally realized to the hard work put in by his predecessors. The contribution of Admiral Sir Arthur Wilson on that occasion, with its continuing emphasis on blockade and amphibious action in the Baltic, showed merely that the Admiralty had not allowed the results of the 1909 inquiry to make the slightest difference to its thinking. This was perhaps the most significant fact to emerge at the meeting of 23rd August 1911; as the appointment of Mr Churchill (described somewhat sourly by Hankey as a 'convert to the military point of view') as First Lord of the Admiralty to change this situation was its most significant result.[86] Otherwise, the meeting did no more than enable the Army and the Navy to deploy before a rather wider audience the arguments they had already used in greater detail two years earlier; without reversing the verdict which their inquisitors had then reached.

This evolution of military policy was, of course, unknown to the public. Sir John Fisher hoped that if it *was* known, the position of the Government would become untenable.[87] Certainly the Radical members of the Cabinet, led by Morley, who had not been invited to the meeting on 23rd August,[88] when they heard what had happened, kicked up a tremendous fuss; in which they were joined by the naturally disgruntled McKenna, who had been so ignominiously ejected from the Admiralty to make room for Churchill. The following autumn they were able to force resolutions through the Cabinet to the effect that 'no communications should take place between the General Staff and the Staffs of other countries which can directly or indirectly commit this country to military or naval intervention;' and that 'such communications, if they relate to concerted action by land or sea, should not be entered into without the previous approval of the Cabinet.'[89] Although they knew nothing for certain, they suspected what was going on and did not like it.

The following year, 1912, provided the dissident Ministers with the opportunity to make a far more public and effective protest. The focus this time was the Royal Navy. Fisher had already carried out a radical redeployment of its dispositions to enable it to meet the growing threat from across the North Sea. He had withdrawn the Pacific, South Atlantic and North American squadrons altogether, amalgamated the Australian, Chinese and East Indian squadrons into a single Eastern Fleet in Singapore, and transformed the old Home Fleet of 8 battleships into a new Channel Fleet 18 battleships strong, which could be further reinforced by an Atalantic Fleet based on Gibraltar. In 1906 a new Home Fleet was created in addition to the Channel Fleet; and in 1909 all vessels in home waters were united in the Home Fleet, 24 battleships strong, to which the Atlantic Fleet, whose principal base had moved to Dover, could bring a further reinforcement of 6 capital ships.[90] In 1912 Churchill, in response to the German supplementary Navy Law of that year, determined to take this concentration a stage further by withdrawing the Mediterranean Fleet from Malta to Gibraltar whence it could support the Home Fleet; leaving Britain's interests in the Mediterranean to be protected by the cruiser squadrons which was all that remained at Malta and, it was generally assumed, by her friends—though not yet her Allies—the French.

This unleashed a storm in which Radicals, Conservatives, Liberals, Imperialists, soldiers, sailors and even diplomats joined. Liberals and radicals objected because of the alliance it implied with France. Conservatives objected because no such alliance yet existed. The Foreign Office objected because the withdrawal of the British naval presence in the Mediterranean would reduce British influence on Turkey, Italy and Spain. The War Office objected because it would render more precarious the position of the garrisons of Cyprus, Egypt and Malta.[91] But most disturbed of all was the Imperial lobby. Lord Roberts put forward its views with comparative moderation in a private letter to Churchill: 'the importance,' he stated 'of showing that we are determined to maintain unimpaired our position in the Mediterranean and Egypt is an incalculable advantage from the point of view of India, for were we once to become seriously embroiled with Turkey, a feeling of unrest would certainly spread to the Mahomedans in India, and this would complicate our defensive arrangements to a dangerous extent.'[92] Lord Esher expressed himself more extravagantly:

Great Britain stands today [he told Mr Balfour on 1st July 1912] at the parting of her Imperial way . . . Britain either is not or is one of the Great Powers of the World. Her position in this respect depends solely upon sea command, and sea command on the Mediterranean. . . . We should be mad to entangle ourselves in a continental strife on land. Our medium is the ocean way. . . . This Mediterranean question is the vital essence of our being.[93]

In the face of the campaign mounted by this powerful if ill-assorted coalition—in the course of which we find the Radicals leading the demand for yet higher spending on the navy, to make it independent of foreign associates[94]—Churchill had to give ground; and on 4th July 1912 the Committee of Imperial Defence resolved that, subject to maintaining 'a reasonable margin of superior strength ready and available in home waters,' there should be kept 'available for Mediterranean purposes, and based on a Mediterranean

port, a battle fleet equal to a one-power Mediterranean standard, excluding France.'[95] The Navy's subsequent inability
to carry out these rather contradictory instructions escaped
public notice. It is this affair, rather than that of the British
Expeditionary Force, which provides the historian with the
fullest illustration, in private and official documents, in
Parliament and in the press, of the arguments for and
against Britain's involvement in continental warfare, and of
the prejudices and preconceptions which lay behind them.

What, in conclusion, was the impact of this reorientation of
British defence policy on the Empire as a whole? How was
the need for the concentration and control of all Imperial
forces which it implied to be reconciled with the desire of
the Dominions (as we must now call them) to preserve their
autonomy and to control their own armed forces; to say
nothing of the continuing preoccupation of Australia with
her own defensive requirements, and the determination of
Sir Wilfred Laurier's government in Canada to remain aloof
from the 'vortex of militarism' that was Europe—a determination which Laurier voiced as eloquently at the Imperial
Conference in 1907 as he had in 1902?

In principle the dilemma remained insoluble. In practice it
was very largely resolved by the remarkable change in the
attitude of the Dominions themselves which took place in
1909 as a result of the 'dreadnought crisis'. During that year
Australian, New Zealand, Canadian, and South African
public opinion was stirred by much the same strong if unpredictable current of concern as had galvanized it during
the Boer and the Crimean Wars: the conviction that, in
spite of everything, the destinies of their own countries remained bound up with that of Great Britain. New Zealand
and the Malay States offered dreadnoughts immediately, and

the Australian government after a brief delay. The Canadian offer of three came only three years later, after Laurier's government had fallen, and in the last resort the opposition was able to kill it off in Parliament.[96] But at the Imperial Conference of 1911 even Laurier spoke in very different terms from those he had used four years earlier. While still insisting on Canada's right to remain neutral if Great Britain was involved in war, he stated:

> If England were engaged today in such a war as, I would not say would imperil her existence, but a war which would put her on her mettle and force her citizens to be anxious, immediately Canada would step forward, I have no doubt at all of that, to go to the rescue and contribute ...in every... way in her power.[97]

And he did not take issue with Sir Edward Grey when the British Foreign Secretary expounded, with a frankness which might have astounded the House of Commons, his view of the connection between the European Balance of Power and the requirements of Imperial Defence. Should any Power or group of Powers in Europe, Grey then pointed out, successfully pursue a Napoleonic policy; and if 'while that policy was going on we were appealed to for help and sat by and looked on and did nothing, then the result would be one great combination in Europe outside which we would be left without a friend.' Against such a combination it would be hardly possible to maintain command of the sea; and

> if control of the sea was lost, it would not only be the end of the British Empire as far as we are concerned, but all the Dominions would be separated from us, never to be rejoined; because the control of the seas, once having passed to a great European power, would never be allowed to return again; and not only would the Dominions be parted

from us, but they would also be separated entirely from one another.[98]

Command of the seas and the maintenance of a European balance were in fact, not alternative policies as both Imperialists and Radicals would have liked to believe, but interdependent; and their understanding of this played at last some part in the readiness with which the Dominions allowed themselves to be sucked into the whirlpool of European politics in August 1914.

3 The Triumph of Empire, 1914–1919

From 1909 the plans of the British Army, and after 1911 the plans of the Royal Navy, were based on the assumption that a German attack on Belgium or France would be a *casus belli* for Britain; and that in that event the British Expeditionary Force would take its place on the left flank of the French Armies. This assumption derived, as we saw in the last chapter, from the political calculation that British security demanded that the balance of power in Europe should not be destroyed by the victory of the German Empire and its allies over the forces of France and Russia; and from the military calculation that the presence of the British Expeditionary Force at what was assumed to be the decisive point would be just sufficient to balance the numerical superiority which the invading German Armies might be expected to enjoy. Further, to get them to that point in time would require careful preliminary preparations which would virtually eliminate all alternative options.

Asquith and his associates had not cared and possibly not dared to reveal either set of calculations to the British public, to Parliament, or even to all their colleagues in the Cabinet. When the moment came for the plans of their military advisers to be put into effect they found themselves in an embarrassing predicament. From this embarrassment they were rescued, first by the German invasion of Belgium, which enabled them to justify British intervention on grounds not of power-politics but of public law that commanded the support of the overwhelming majority of their countrymen; and second, by the failure of the critics of the agreed military plans to come up with any equally well-prepared and closely-reasoned alternatives. The decision taken on 5th August to implement the plans on which the General Staff had been working for the past five years was harshly criticized, even at the time, as a departure from Britain's traditional strategy. Lord Esher and Colonel Hankey, staunch supporters of maritime power, wrote about it in almost identical terms. 'By the precipitate alignment of our army to that of the French,' wrote Esher, in his diary for 6th August 1914, 'we forego the advantages of sea power.' Hankey had already, after the Committee of Imperial Defence meeting of 23rd August 1911, written a dissenting memorandum pointing out that 'if the army has been committed to the centre of the campaign at the outset of war, all possibility of influencing the course of the war in . . . a manner which sea power alone can render possible, disappears, and the great advantage of sea power is to a great extent thrown away.'[99]

The fact that the strategy adopted was to result in a permanent commitment to the Western Front, and that the fighting on that front led to four years of appalling slaughter, has led many historians of great eminence to add their voices to these criticisms. Yet what alternatives were really open at the time? There was the advice given at the War Council of 5th August by General Sir Douglas Haig, that they should wait for two or three months to see how things went and to enable 'the immense resources of the Empire' to be developed.[100] But this would mean ignoring the advice of the General Staff, backed by all the conventional wisdom of the day, that the issue was likely to be settled by a series of great clashes on the frontier as rapidly and decisively as it had been in 1870. (And they were not very far wrong.) Within the two or three months postulated by Haig, the Germans might well control the entire coast of France and Belgium. There was the alternative mooted at the same meeting by Sir John French, of a landing at Antwerp to threaten the northern flank of the German armies; a possibility already considered by von Schlieffen in formulating his plan and dismissed with the contemptuous comment that the British Expeditionary Force would be more securely billetted in that fortress than on their own island, and present even less of a threat.[101] As for more distant expeditions to the Baltic, one can only say that those who still contemplated them had as yet little idea of the logistical problems of transporting and disembarking modern armies in the face of opposition and of maintaining them in what would in all probability be a prolonged and bitter campaign. It is far from clear that in August 1914 any of the alternatives that sea power made possible were really preferable to intervention at what was certainly the point of greatest logistical simplicity and, arguably, that of greatest military effect.

No one could foretell, either, that the commitment in France was going to grow quite so inexorably. (And no one can be sure that a commitment anywhere else would not have grown just as inexorably and, in the hands of the same commanders, have produced any more effective results with any less loss of life.) The orders which Sir John French received as Commander in Chief of the British Expeditionary Force were indeed quite meticulously drafted to limit that commitment:

The numerical strength of the British Force [ran his instructions] and its contingent reinforcements is strictly limited, and with this consideration kept steadily in view it will be obvious that the greatest care must be exercised towards a minimum of losses and wastage. Therefore, while effort must be made to coincide most sympathetically with the plans and wishes of our Ally, the gravest consideration will devolve on you as to participation in forward movements where large bodies of French troops are not engaged and where your force may be unduly exposed to attack.[102]

French, it will be remembered, interpreted these instructions so literally that, on 1st September, Lord Kitchener felt it necessary to intervene in person to prevent British forces being withdrawn from action altogether.[103] Thereafter the British Army was caught up in the first battle of Ypres and had to be substantially reinforced if it was not to be completely destroyed. But once the fighting had died down, the British Government, in January 1915, began to reconsider its strategy on the assumption that all options were still open—and indeed that several more had now been opened by the belligerency of Turkey. On 13th January the War Council resolved that 'if the position in the Western theatre becomes in the Spring one of stalemate, British troops should be despatched to another theatre and another objective.'[104]

Another objective did indeed offer itself, and on 25th April British troops landed on the Gallipoli peninsula. The commitment of the British Expeditionary Force to France had not, after all, foreclosed the options provided by maritime power. By June 1915, after the failure of the attacks at Neuve Chapelle in March and Festubert in May, it was increasingly clear that the position in the Western theatre had indeed become one of stalemate. It was now, perhaps even more than in August 1914, that the real choice had to be made between retaining freedom of action and accepting total commitment to the Western Front. Large scale detach-

ments from the Western Front to the Mediterranean might
still, as Churchill and later Lloyd George so powerfully
argued, have made it possible to defeat the enemy's allies;
but it would have been at risk of losing at least one of our
own. Throughout the summer the German armies were
hammering the Eastern Front and by autumn had inflicted
on the Russian armies nearly two million casualties. By
August Kitchener had come to the conclusion that if no
offensive was launched on the Western Front to relieve
pressure in the East, Russia would collapse; and that if the
British failed to participate in such an offensive there was a
real danger that a government would come into power in
France that would negotiate a compromise peace. We must
therefore, he informed Haig, on 19th August, 'act with all
our energy and do our utmost to help the French, even
though, by so doing, we suffered very heavy casualties indeed.'[105] It was with that decision that the total commitment
of British resources to the Western Front really began.

If we are to condemn that commitment, we must distin-
guish three elements in it: operational, strategic and political.
One may accept its necessity on strategic and political
grounds without endorsing the manner in which the
operations to which it led were actually conducted. By
autumn 1915 the original highly-trained British Expeditionary Force had disappeared, and in the New Armies which
replaced it all ranks, from the Commander in Chief to
private soldiers, were learning, from the beginning and at
hideous cost, a new kind of war which baffled even ex-
perienced continental armies. It was only in 1918 that even
the Germans developed effective techniques of attack under
conditions of trench warfare. The strategic argument, that
more effective support could have been given to Britain's
allies at less cost by intervention on other fronts in other

parts of Europe, is superficially attractive; yet it has never
been conclusively shown that the terrain of South or South-
East Europe—that famous 'soft underbelly'—offered battle-
fields which German forces could not have reached as
quickly and defended as stubbornly as they did their lines
on the Western Front, and where the inexperienced British
armies could have attacked with any greater chance of
success. As for the political argument, it is seldom explicitly raised, but it is this: would it have mattered to
Britain if Germany *had* defeated France and Russia and
established a new Napoleonic Empire? Was not seven
hundred thousand dead too high a price to pay to prevent a
German hegemony in Europe?

So far as I have been able to discover, no statesman or
public figure in Britain of any party after the war was prepared to face this question so honestly as did some of their
French colleagues and answer with an unequivocal yes: the
price was too high. Some—including the bulk of left-wing
thinkers—escaped from the problem by denying the whole
validity of the concept of the balance of power. Others—
the frank appeasers like Geoffrey Dawson and Lord Lothian
—ignored it. They saw no difficulty in the coexistence of
Britain and a Germany dominating at least Central Europe
and extending its power indefinitely to the East. And those
military writers who, like Admiral Sir Herbert Richmond
and Captain Sir Basil Liddell Hart, continued to plead for
more flexible strategies, never really faced the disagreeable
fact that such flexibility depended for its success on a contin-
nental ally being prepared to accept the sufferings which the
British could avoid; and that neither the military strength
nor the political patience of such Allies was inexhaustible.
Foch warned Henry Wilson in February 1915: 'You English
must not invite a long war by dilatory action. We French

cannot go on for years so send everyone you can as fast as you can.'[106] Kitchener's decision in August was in fact prompted by the realization that not only Russia but France was within sight of the end of her moral and material resources. The same revelation was to result in the total reversal which British military policy was to undergo during the winter of 1938–1939.

What, meanwhile, of the British Empire? Once the German naval squadron in the Pacific Ocean under the Graf von Spee had been destroyed at the Battle of the Falkland Isles, the Dominions were confronted with no serious problems of local defence. Their Anglo-Saxon populations had responded to the outbreak of war with predictable, if, in the eyes of posterity, inexplicable enthusiasm and flocked to the recruiting offices. India also responded with a zest which delighted and rather surprised the officials who had been watching the activities of the Indian nationalists with growing alarm. Sir Francis Younghusband wrote of India, in the semi-official history, *The Empire at War*: 'In a flash she realized all that England, all that the Empire meant. She thrilled with the joy of battling by the side of England and by the side of Great Britain's sturdy offspring, in the great and glorious cause.'[107] That was probably pitching it a bit high; but certainly India was to be in no sense a liability during the First World War, even if the state of organization and training of the Indian Army limited—as the Mesopotamian campaign showed—its value as an asset.

To improve matters still further, fate had provided the British Empire with almost the ideal adversary. It was against Turkey that Imperial forces could be most easily concentrated. Mesopotamia, with dissident tribes over the border and its valuable oil supplies, lay within the traditional field of action of the Government of India. Egypt was a natural entrepôt not only for Indian but for Antipodean and South African forces on their way to Europe, and the British already had there a sophisticated military base from which large-scale operations could be mounted. Finally, in the Eastern Mediterranean, British naval power could furnish both the mobility and the capacity for exercising direct political pressure that the protagonists of a maritime strategy had always attributed to it: capabilities as relevant to the disturbed political situation in South-East Europe as they were to Turkey's restive possessions in Asia. In the First World War as in the Second, the positions which the British had occupied in the Middle East, mainly to safeguard her route to India, in fact proved valuable primarily as a base from which they could attack the most vulnerable of their adversaries.

Still, such operations had their own peculiar perils. When Turkey first entered the war, British officials feared the effect which a *jihad*, a Holy War, proclaimed by the Caliph might have upon the Moslem subjects of the British Crown. In fact the Moslems found no more difficulty than most men in reconciling their secular and their religious loyalties. But within a few months, when British forces began to suffer humiliating defeats, a graver danger became apparent.

On 24th November 1915 Colonel Hankey had to record in his diary the simultaneous news of the repulse of Anglo-Indian forces at Ctesiphon in Mesopotamia; of the failure of the Anglo-French attacks at Salonica; and of the impending evacuation of Imperial troops at Gallipoli.

Combined [he wrote] these three misadventures will destroy the last vestige of our prestige, upon which our Eastern Empire depends; it will ruin our hopes among the

Arabs, in Persia and probably in China; it will place our position in India and possibly in Egypt in peril.[108]

It was a fear which Kitchener, with his lifetime's experience in the Near East and in India, very deeply shared;[109] and the result was to divide the Cabinet and delay still further any decision about the evacuation of the Dardanelles. It was clear even at this stage of the war that the Empire might prove as much a source of weakness as of strength.

All being well, the Turkish theatre in 1915 certainly provided obvious opportunities for action which not even the most dedicated 'Westerner' could afford to neglect. If the campaigns in Mesopotamia and the Dardanelles had been conducted with greater skill and attended with better fortune they might indeed have forced on the Germans a palpable diversion of strength to prevent their ally from collapsing completely. As it was, their failure provided arguments against further 'sideshows' which the most dedicated 'Easterner' found difficult to answer—at least until another disastrous year had passed on the Western Front; and on the Western Front the strength of the British Empire was therefore concentrated. Indian infantry units had to be withdrawn from France after the Battle of Loos in autumn 1915 to save them from another bitter winter in the trenches; but the Anzac Corps took their place the following spring, reinforced by a further Australian division, in time for the Battle of the Somme in July 1916. The Canadians had already had their baptism of fire at the second Battle of Ypres in spring 1915, and when the attack on the Somme opened they had an entire Army Corps in France and Flanders. By the time that battle ended the dominion forces had between them suffered some 60,000 casualties and were expressing their opinions about British military leadership in colourful terms.[110]

The increasing contribution which the dominion forces were making on the Western Front, apart from its military value, was to have also interesting political consequences. It was to make possible the remarkable coalition between Lloyd George and the High Imperialists which came to power in London at the end of 1916 and was thereafter to supervise the strategic conduct of the war. Throughout 1915 and 1916 the Prime Ministers of Canada and Australia had been pressing in vain for some right of consultation about the conduct of operations in which the lives of their fellow-countrymen were being disposed of by British commanders with what at times appeared to them to be callous incompetence; receiving little in return but assurances, in Mr Hughes's bitter words, of the 'almost superhuman ability' of the men in charge of the war.[111] At the same time Lord Milner, a figure brooding apart from the hurly-burly of party politics and, it may be said, of political realities, was trying to reanimate the defunct idea of a single Imperial Cabinet which would guide the affairs of 'a single British State embodying all the scattered portions of our race throughout the world;' a view which his henchman Amery boiled down into more immediate and concrete terms: 'The urgent thing,' he told Hughes, 'is to get the half dozen or so strongest men in the Empire together to make sure, first, of winning the war, and then of not allowing that victory to be thrown away in the peace negotiations.'[112]

There had been little in Lloyd George's career up till then to suggest that he would have the slightest sympathy with any such idea. But in the political circumstances of December 1916 the Imperialists were, oddly enough, his natural allies. The great Imperial proconsuls, Milner and Curzon, carried the respect of the Conservative party without being in the least dependent on their support. Their interest in the efficient conduct of the war was not tempered by any great concern for the views of Horatio Bottomley or Lord Beaverbrook, or the Harmsworth press. Their presence in the War Cabinet did much to lift Lloyd George above the political battle and give even that arch-politician, to the limited degree possible, a certain supra-political status.

Even more natural as allies for Lloyd George were the dominion Prime Ministers; political animals like himself, emerging from much the same humble social origins, sharing his exasperation at the apparent arrogance and inefficiency of the British High Command. Small wonder, then, that within a few days of coming into office as Prime Minister, Lloyd George, on Milner's advice, should have summoned an Imperial Conference. The dominion representatives, once assembled, quickly disposed of Milner. Led by Smuts they made clear their total opposition to his ideas of a Federal Empire. They were *not* an Empire at all and not even British, said Smuts mistily, but a Commonwealth of Nations—'a system of States and not a stationary but a dynamic and evolving system, always going forward to new destinies;'[113] a convenient formula into which absolutely anything could, and has, been made to fit. But they equally gratified Lloyd George by their outspoken criticisms of the military conduct of the war hitherto. The Conference was therefore given a kind of permanence by the creation of an Imperial War Cabinet, which has been well described as 'in effect a session of the British War Cabinet with dominion members and other members in attendance.'[114] A few months later, in June 1917, this body devolved the day-to-day conduct of the war on to a small Committee on War Policy consisting simply of Lloyd George, Milner, Curzon and Smuts. And with Milner came the most formidable young men of the Kindergarten and the Round Table:

Philip Kerr as private secretary to the Prime Minister, Leo Amery as an associate to the rather apprehensive Colonel Hankey in the Cabinet secretariat, others camping out in the garden of 10 Downing Street to run the war and plan the peace.[115]

The campaign on the Western Front had now to be justified to a small group of able and independent-minded men who listened to the proposals which the High Command put before them for further offensives with open scepticism.[116] They did not however quite have the self-confidence to veto those plans and so avert the blood-letting of the ensuing twelve months. The British conduct of operations during this period, which included not only the Passchendaele offensive but the rout of the Fifth Army the following spring, did nothing to restore and little to merit the confidence of the Dominions whose forces, during the Passchendaele campaign alone, lost nearly 50,000 men. But their protests enabled Lloyd George in June 1918 to establish the 'Committee of Prime Ministers' which thereafter closely supervised the conduct of operations in France.[117] The Dominions may have rejected Milner's federalist formula, and still have been unbendingly hostile to any political involvement in Europe; but if they could not trust the British to conduct the war for them, there was no alternative to taking it over themselves. Thus it was that by the end of the war the Dominion Prime Ministers had virtually assumed joint responsibility for the conduct of the war; and that responsibility was, through the British Empire Delegation at the Paris Conference, to extend into the making of the peace.

The Imperial War Cabinet in 1917 regarded the Western Front as little more than a disagreeable necessity. A policy-making group consisting of Curzon, Milner, and Smuts, and serviced by such men as Leo Amery and Mark Sykes, was not likely to give to the European theatre any larger priority than it could help. Lloyd George had already, in December 1916 and February 1917, relaxed the moratorium imposed at the end of 1915 on all operations in the Middle East, and authorized offensives against Palestine and Baghdad.[118] In July 1917 the Imperial War Cabinet ordered General Allenby, the new Commander in Egypt, to 'strike the Turks as hard as possible.' This he very successfully did, obtaining Jerusalem for the British public as their hoped-for Christmas present by the end of the year.[119] Early in 1918 the War Policy Committee despatched Smuts, with the ubiquitous Amery to advise him, to see how this success could best be exploited; and Amery for one had never lost sight of the possibilities of war as an instrument of imperial policy. It was at about this time that he wrote for Lloyd George the highly suggestive memorandum on British war aims which he reprints in his Memoirs:

> We have battled and will continue to battle our hardest for the common cause in Europe. But on behalf of that cause, as well as in defence of our existence, we shall find ourselves compelled to complete the liberation of the Arabs, to make secure the independence of Persia and if we can of Armenia, to protect tropical Africa from German economic and military exploitation. All these objects are desirable in themselves and don't become less so because they increase the general sphere of British influence and afford a strategical security which will enable that Southern British World which runs from Cape Town through Cairo, Baghdad and Calcutta to Sydney and Wellington to go about its peaceful business without constant fear of German aggression.[120]

The establishment of British influence and where necessary British rule on the ruins of the Ottoman Empire was thus a necessary part, the keystone in the arch, of this Grand Design; and into this design how smoothly there fitted the decision, embodied in the formula which was publicly announced by Balfour but drafted by Milner and Amery, to establish in Palestine, under British protection, a national home for the Jewish race![121]

Political scientists may well argue that the main cause of the expansion of Empires is not zeal for territorial conquest or search for commercial gain, but the fear that an adversary might get in first. In 1918, certainly, it was this fear that led certain elements in London to advocate advances which would have brought within the *limes* of the Empire, not simply the greater part of the Middle East, but considerable areas of Central Asia, from the Caucasus to Turkestan, as well. 'From the left bank of the Don to India is our preserve,' wrote Henry Wilson, now Chief of the Imperial General Staff.[122] In December 1918 the General Staff was urging on the War Cabinet the importance of controlling the Caucasus in order to protect the overland route to India; and Curzon, as might have been expected, added his wholehearted support:

> The whole experience of this war [Curzon declared to a Cabinet Committee] has taught us the supreme importance of this region, with a view to the countries further east over which it is essential in the interests of India and of our Empire, that we should exercise some measure of political control. A hostile force in possession of this region of the Caucasus would turn the flank of the British position in Asia.[123]

Curzon's audience was unsympathetic. Its reaction was probably that expressed by Balfour, who complained mildly:

Every time I come to a discussion—at intervals of, say, five years—I find there is a new sphere which we have got to guard, which is supposed to protect the gateways of India. Those gateways are getting further and further away from India, and I do not know how far west they are going to be brought by the General Staff.

Curzon replied, a little defensively, 'We are talking of staying in the Caucasus to put the people on their feet there;' to which Lord Robert Cecil answered: 'You ought not to be taken in by that phrase. We get there so often, and we always remain.'[124]

Yet under the circumstances of the time, the views of the General Staff were understandable enough. The Ottoman Empire was not the only power in Eastern Europe on the verge of collapse. By the end of 1917 the Russian front had entirely disintegrated, leaving behind it a condition not so much of revolution as of simple anarchy. During the ensuing year the speed of the German advance across the Ukraine towards the Caucasus was limited only by problems of supply. Beyond the Caucasus their agents were believed to be busy in Trans-Caspia, and were certainly busy in Persia. At the same time the Turks, seeking in the Turanian lands to the north-east compensation for the loss of their Arabian possessions, were moving on the Caspian from the west. In the total confusion left by the collapse of the Russian Empire, anything seemed possible, and intelligence reports to the War Cabinet painted nightmare prospects. Germany, these suggested, was aiming at control of Caucasia, of Armenia, of Persia and Mesopotamia. She would establish submarine bases on the Indian Ocean. Under her protection the Turks would create a huge Islamic State out of the thirteen million Turkish-speaking inhabitants of Central Asia. 'As the policy of the future,' warned one report, dated 11 May 1918, 'Germany will be in a position to threaten British rule in India with a Mahomedan invasion from the North or later on, if German government is established throughout Central Asia, with an actual attack by German armies.'[125] In India all alarm-bells rang. 'The opinion of those in high places at Simla,' wrote one senior officer, 'was that it needed the appearance of but a detachment of German or Turkish troops on the Northern frontiers of Afghanistan to precipitate a *jihad* against us;' and in April 1918 Mr Lloyd George warned the Viceroy that 'India must equip itself on an even greater scale than at present to be the bulwark which will save Asia from the tide of oppression and disorder which it is the object of the enemy to achieve.'[126]

The events of 1917–18, like those of 1941–42, thus gave new and disconcerting emphasis to the connection which Sir Edward Grey had spelled out for the Dominion Prime Ministers in 1911, between the balance of power in Europe and the defence-needs of the British imperial system. Grey had stressed the naval aspects of this connection: the inability of the Royal Navy to hold the seas against a hostile Continental coalition. But no less a danger was presented by the prospect of a great industrialized European power expanding indefinitely eastward, absorbing the economic resources of South Russia, taking over Russia's part in the Great Game, creating a power-base invulnerable to maritime pressure which would pose a standing threat to Britain's Eastern Empire. The prevention of such a situation had been the most compelling argument in 1915 in favour of an unlimited commitment of British forces to tie down German strength in the West. The same reasoning was to appear again in the arguments for a Second Front twenty-seven years later. But by the beginning of 1918 all the sacrifices on the Western Front seemed vain. Russia had collapsed none the less.

In July 1918 Sir Henry Wilson, as Chief of the Imperial General Staff, tried to draw up a balanced picture of the situation, and was appalled by what he saw.[127] Even the advent of American forces on the Western Front, he argued, would not affect the issue. 'If the Germans are allowed another year to consolidate their power in Russia and Asia, they will have time so to exploit the vast reservoir of raw material and manpower as will enable them, to a great extent, to counter the increase in Allied strength in the West, while their prospects after the war will be immeasurably brighter.' There could thus be no question of abandoning the conquered territories of Palestine and Mesopotamia:

We have to remember [wrote Wilson] that in the next war we may be fighting Germany alone and unaided, while she will have Turkey and perhaps part of Russia, if not on her side, at least under her thumb. In such circumstances Germany, with no preoccupation in Europe, could concentrate great armies against Egypt or India by her overland routes, which are beyond the reach of our sea power.

Unless her hold on Russia could be shaken, he argued, she would be able to exploit Russian manpower and economic resources; and

with this double increment of recuperative power, Germany will be practically independent of maritime blockade and will be able completely to outstrip the rest of Europe in the reconstruction of their economic and military resources. Thus at no distant date Germany will be in a position again to threaten the peace of civilization and consummate the dominion of half the world.

This picture, it must be admitted, took little account of the political problems which Germany would face in establishing such a dominion, and none of the logistical difficulties involved in transporting 'great armies' across the distances involved. Still, Wilson's analysis was not all that remote from the grandiose plans being entertained by Ludendorff and his entourage at the time; or from the actual achievement of German armies a quarter of a century later.

It was to counter this danger that British forces, in 1918, were pushed northwards from Mesopotamia into the Caucasus, from South Persia towards the Caspian and from India into Trans-Caspia;[128] that such desperate attempts were made to persuade the Japanese to send forces through Siberia to recreate some kind of Eastern Front; and that the British Government, by its support for various local regimes in South-East Russia which gave some prospect of restoring order and of offering resistance to the Germans, allowed itself to be sucked in to the wars of intervention in the Soviet Union which were to drag so pointlessly on after the German collapse a few months later.[129] It was an experience which, combined with the fears of creeping Bolshevism into which the German threat imperceptibly merged, strengthened the British determination to abandon as little as they could of the territories conquered in the Middle East by their advancing armies. 'The territorial settlement,' as Max Beloff has written, 'was the product not of planned expansion but of the impossibility of restoring the defeated Empire, including the Turkish Empire, and of the unwillingness to see Soviet influence extend more widely than need be;' to which one should add a prudent determination to retain control of the oil-bearing districts round the Persian Gulf.[130]

For the rest it may be said of Great Britain in the Middle

East as it was of Maria Theresa in the partitions of Poland: *'elle pleurait, mais prenait toujours.'* In Mesopotamia Sir Percy Cox set about creating a British controlled State 'with an Arab façade' which was a virtual, and all too natural extension of the British Empire in India. Persia was not to be be allowed to relapse into its own genial anarchy, but to be made to accept British military and financial control.[131] Palestine was to be retained as a necessary buffer for Egypt, and to keep the French out; although at least one of the British statesmen responsible realized what this might involve.

> There is not [observed Sir Robert Cecil, at a Cabinet Committee on 5th December] going to be any great catch in it . . . we shall simply keep the peace between the Arabs and the Jews. We are not going to get anything out of it. Whoever goes there will have a poor time.[132]

In the same spirit of weary resignation Britain was prepared, in December 1918, to accept a Protectorate over the Caucasian Republics: provisionally, 'only in the last resort, and reluctantly if pressed to do so.' Into these discussions Mr Balfour tried to introduce a note of realism.

> We talk [he said on 16 December 1918] of huge protectorates all over the place. I am really frightened at the responsibilities which we are taking upon ourselves, because who has to bear the responsibilities? Two offices in the main—the Treasury and the War Office. . . . Where are they going to find the men and the money for these things?[133]

Balfour might well ask. The Treasury could not find the money and the War Office could certainly not provide the men. The inhabitants of the Caucasus and of Persia were therefore left to work out their own salvation. The remaining responsibilities in Egypt, Palestine and Mesopotamia were to prove more than enough for a shrunken British Army to handle on a shrunken British budget.

Nevertheless as a result of the First World War the British Empire reached its greatest territorial extent, and the peak of its influence on world politics. Had victory come a year earlier, before France had recovered from the catastrophe of the Nivelle offensive and before American strength had begun to make itself felt, that influence would no doubt have been greater still; for as Lloyd George was shrewdly aware, there is a direct correlation between the contribution which a State makes to the final victory and its voice in the making of the peace. Gallant sacrifices early on in the war, the invisible contributions of sea power, all this counted for very little, in European eyes, in comparison with the number of victorious bayonets present at the final battles. Hankey observed in August 1918 the jealousy with which Lloyd George watched the growth of Clemenceau's prestige as a result of the recent French victories and his apprehension at 'the position President Wilson will achieve when the peace comes, with enormous American armies on the Western Front. He feels that . . . between American success and French prestige, he and Great Britain will at the peace conference cut a poor figure.' And two months later he noted that Smuts was 'very keen that we should make peace this year when the victory is due mainly to British arms, and not next year when it may be due mainly to American.'[134]

Smuts was indeed, as his biographer had pointed out, a statesman who bore the stamp of Cavour. But it is not only those concerned with the preservation and extension of British power who may wonder whether, if the war had ended in November 1917, a peace might not have been made which owed less to the unworldliness of Wilson or to the vindictiveness of Clemenceau; and whether, if that had been the case, the sacrifices of the Western Front might not have appeared so wholly in vain.

4 The Locarno Era, 1919–1931

By the end of the First World War the British Empire had thus reached its apogee. That 'Southern British World' of which Amery had written did indeed now stretch in an unbroken crescent from the Cape through Cairo to Jerusalem, and on through Baghdad to Karachi, Calcutta, Singapore, Sydney and Wellington. The Dominions had paid, at Gallipoli and Vimy Ridge, the price which entitled them to act as fully independent members of the international system, and their presence at the Peace Conference in Paris increased yet further the authority with which the British voice spoke in world affairs. This, surely, should have been the British Empire's finest hour?

And yet somehow it was not. The victory itself was too ambiguous. The sentiments evoked by the unveiling of the Cenotaph in Whitehall, a symbol not of triumph but of mourning; by the burial of the Unknown Warrior in Westminster Abbey; by the repeated intoning of that most melancholy of all hymns 'Oh God our Help in Ages Past'; by the inscription on regimental colours of those dreadful names, Ypres, Festubert, Loos, Somme, Passchendaele: these feelings were not ones of unalloyed pride. Some time during these celebrations there was formulated that simple phrase which the people not only of Great Britain but of the Dominions resolved should be the epitaph of their million-odd war dead: Never Again. Unfortunately, it was to be

more than an epitaph; it was to be a policy—and one which
was to have disastrous results.

In fact the characteristics which made the British Empire
seem so strong in 1919 were in almost every respect elements
of weakness rather than of strength. Sanderson's 'gouty
giant' had become a brontosaurus with huge, vulnerable
limbs which the central nervous system had little capacity to
protect, direct or control. Less than ever were the Dominions
now prepared to allow their foreign or defence policy to be
laid down in London, or to envisage their armed forces in
any future conflict coming under the control of British commanders. The experience of the war had strengthened isolationist sentiment everywhere; in Canada perhaps most of all.
There, a figure more isolationist even than Wilfred Laurier,
Mackenzie King, became Prime Minister in 1921 and remained so with few interruptions until the Second World
War: a man, in the words of a Canadian historian, with 'a
marked aversion to the military life and the military mind,
whose working he failed to understand and whose virtues he
ignored.'[135] At the Imperial Conference of 1923, King made
his policy quite explicit: 'We should not do anything,' he
said, 'which will create in the minds [of new immigrants]
the idea that because they are settling in the part of North
America which is British they are running risks and in-
curring obligations with respect to situations arising in parts
remote from America, which they would not have if they
were south of the line.'[136] Canadian attitudes, he implied, if
not Canadian policy, would henceforth be shaped by those
of the United States rather than by those of the United
Kingdom. As his representative at Geneva put it in a
famous phrase: 'We live in a fire-proof house, far from in-
flammable materials.'[137] King was determined to keep it
that way.

The attitude of South Africa was little different, complicated as it was by a conflict of loyalties only precariously resolved by the Union which Smuts worked so hard to preserve. Smuts himself took back to South Africa from the Paris Conference a bitter hatred, if not of all things European, at least of all things French; which under the circumstances was to amount to much the same thing. 'Whenever the suggestion came up of any commitment to France,' wrote his biographer, 'he showed himself just as much an isolationist as any politician of the Middle West.'[138] He opposed the Locarno Treaties 'almost to the last ditch,' while at the same time denying to the League of Nations any kind of coercive powers—until the Abyssinian crisis, by when it was too late. South Africa and Canada, it might be said, used their new and dearly-bought membership of the international system to contract out of it.

As for Australia and New Zealand, their reluctance to risk further involvement in Europe was not the result of any feeling that their own houses were fire-proof; far from it. They knew they were only too vulnerable and that the Pacific was a highly combustible area. The contribution which they had made at Gallipoli was a debt which London might one day have to repay with heavy interest. If Canada and South Africa had withdrawn their deposits, the Antipodean Dominions represented new and heavy liabilities on the Imperial account.

That account was already choked with liabilities, and every square yard which accrued to the Empire as a result of the Peace Treaties seemed to bring more. In July 1920 a General Staff appreciation of 'the Military Liabilities of the Empire'[139] gave a dismal list which opened inevitably with Ireland, where three divisions were pinned down and a fourth would soon be needed. It went on to the occupation force in a near-chaotic Germany; the two divisions guarding the Straits and Constantinople; Egypt, which had just erupted in violent insurrection; Mesopotamia, which was erupting at that very moment and which might need to be defended against Turkey's claim to Mosul; Palestine, where, the document noted presciently, 'the Arabs are developing a national spirit which ultimately may not prove to be advantageous to us;' Persia, where two brigades were bogged down defending their own communications; and India— where, the appreciation noted, large numbers of the inhabitants had now been trained to the use of arms and were being advised by agitators whom to use them against. If there was no longer any overt danger of Russian invasion, 'its place [has] been taken by Bolshevik activities, and while from a military point of view the danger may be regarded as less imposing, it is perhaps a more subtle and imminent one.'

This particular danger was evident rather nearer home. 'Nor has Great Britain itself,' the General Staff wrote some six months later in a note for the Cabinet,[140] 'entirely escaped from the effects of revolutionary propaganda acting on the comparatively receptive soil of a highly organized industrial population temporarily affected by war-weariness. Whilst the country is in this condition the Regular Army at home cannot be considered as free to proceed abroad as it was even in the days of the South African War.' 'In sum,' their appreciation concluded rather helplessly, 'our liabilities are so vast, and at the same time so indeterminate, that to assess them must be largely a matter of conjecture.'

Some of the liabilities listed were transitory peace-keeping operations; some, such as Ireland and Persia, were terminated by policies in which prudence was allowed to triumph over that high minded itch for responsibility which, far more than any desire for territorial conquest or economic gain, has got the Anglo-Saxon nations into such trouble in so many parts of the world and keeps them from getting out again. The British people did not prove to be as ripe for revolution as Lenin hoped and the General Staff feared. Yet domestic pressures were to limit British military power quite as effectively as any incipient revolution. The Lloyd George Government recognized them when in 1919 it took the quite deliberate decision that since it could not afford to take risks over domestic issues it must be take them over defence. Public expenditure and taxes were to be cut back to help the economy on to its feet again.[141] As a contribution to this policy of retrenchment, the Services in August 1919 were ordered to draft their estimates 'on the assumption that the British Empire would not be engaged in any great war during the next ten years and no Expeditionary Force is required for the purpose':[142] a reasonable enough assumption under the circumstances, which in the event proved absolutely correct.

In consequence, in 1920 expenditure on the Armed Forces was reduced by more than half, from £604 m. to £292 m., and over the next two years it was reduced by more than half again to £111 m.: a figure round which it was to fluctuate until the first tentative steps in rearmament began in 1935. As a percentage of the Gross National Product this expenditure was no greater than it had been before the war: but in days when taxation had quadrupled and the National Debt increased tenfold, from some £650 m. to £7,500 m., it still seemed too much.[143] In May 1923 a Conservative Chancellor of the Exchequer warned that unless expenditure could be reduced yet further 'the inevitable result will be the stabilization of taxation at something very near to its present level (five shillings in the pound) the consequence of which may easily be the substitution for the present Government of one whose regard for the defence Services is not particularly marked.'[144] The Chancellor in question was Stanley Baldwin. The same reasoning was to lead him, as Prime Minister, to delay the initiation of rearmament a little more than ten years later, as he was to admit in the House of Commons, with 'appalling frankness', on 12th November 1936.[145]

To read through the minutes and memoranda of the Committee of Imperial Defence from its origins in the early part of the century until the eve of the Second World War is to gain a remarkable overall impression of continuity. This is partly, of course, because of the style which Hankey imprinted on the record which he and his assistants kept during the greater part of this period. It is partly because so many of the issues discussed—the defence of India, the Persian Gulf, the Suez Canal, the Navy in the Mediterranean, the Channel Tunnel, relations with the Dominions, the security of the British Isles—provided an unvarying staple fare. And it is partly because several of the leading participants remained on the stage at least until the fall of the Baldwin Administration in 1929; Balfour and Churchill, whose interventions were equally inimitable and enjoyable, foremost among them. But after 1918 the reader becomes conscious of a new sound: the heavy and ominous breathing of a parsimonious and pacific electorate, to the variations in which the ears of British statesmen were increasingly attuned. What the electorate would or would not accept in the way of taxation; in the way of military expenditure; in the way of information about the probability or intensity of air raids; in the way, above all, of military commitments to the continent; this had not been ignored before 1914, but it had not then been discussed with quite such anguished

interest or accepted quite so readily as the final court of jurisdiction as it was by the Baldwin, the MacDonald and even
the Chamberlain administrations. This was obviously a
highly desirable step in the direction of representative
government; yet one can welcome the disappearance from
the political scene of such figures as Lord Curzon and Lord
Milner, with their tendency to regard public opinion
simply as a disagreeable obstacle to their plans for imperial
expansion and consolidation, without being entirely happy
about the readiness of their successors to tailor their policy
to the mood of the electorate instead of working out for
themselves, on the basis of the evidence before them, what
that policy ought to be and risking unpopularity and if
need be electoral defeat in attempting to explain it.

There was in fact a quite terrifying contrast between the
state of the post-war world as British governments perceived
it, and as the British people wished it to be. Throughout the
Empire—particularly in that area of it which extended from
Cairo to Singapore—the winds of nationalist revolt against
European colonial empires were beginning to rise to gale
force. In Europe Germany was openly resentful at the in-
justices of a settlement all the more intolerable in that it
claimed to be based on principles of justice and national
self-determination. Yet if Germany were accorded justice
by the rectification of her frontiers, would this not once
again result in her domination of the Continent, unless her
neighbours once more joined forces against her? And if she
did again dominate the Continent, what security could there
be for a Britain who now for the first time in her history
really *was* vulnerable: not, perhaps to bands of waiters armed
with cudgels and revolvers, but to a form of attack against
which there seemed to be no possible defence: bombardment
from the air?

That danger had been foreseen by the Committee of the Imperial War Cabinet, consisting of Lloyd George and Smuts, which was set up in the aftermath of the German daylight raids on London in summer 1917. 'The day may not be far off,' they had stated in their Report, 'when aerial operations with their devastation of enemy lands and the destruction of industrial and populous centres on a vast scale may become the principal operations of war, to which the older forms of military and naval operations may become secondary and subordinate.'[146] The independent Royal Air Force was established as a direct consequence of that report. Both professional duty and, in an era of rapidly shrinking budgets, a desire for institutional survival combined to induce the Air Staff to remind successive Cabinets of Smuts's words, in season and out of season. In May 1921 the first Chief of the Air Staff, Sir Hugh Trenchard, argued before the Cabinet Standing Sub-Committee on Defence that 'it is only by way of the air that one country can reach the heart of another in the earliest days of war and drive home the fear of personal injury and loss to every individual'; and maintained that 'in the future the danger of air attack would be so great, so insistent and so constant, that the importance of defence against air attack was predominant, and that the control of the defensive measures to meet aerial attack should rest in the hands of the air force.[147]

The Sub-Committee in question was chaired by Balfour; the same man who, twenty years earlier, had been subjected to comparable arguments about the vulnerability of the country to seaborne invasion and who had then coldly rejected them. Now he proved easier to convince. Defence against air attack, he agreed, was 'the most formidable defence problem now before us'.[148] A Sub-Committee of the Committee of Imperial Defence was set up in the spring of

1922 to consider the matter. It examined data available about the effect of air raids during the last war. It assessed the scale of attack which might be launched by the nearest foreign air force—the French—and concluded that after an initial attack with 150 tons of bombs a continuous daily level of 75 tons might be maintained. The Germans in their heaviest raids on London, it pointed out, had dropped only three tons at any one time. 'Railway traffic would be disorganized,' it reported, 'food supplies would be interrupted, and it is probable that after being subjected for several weeks to the strain of such an attack the population would be so demoralized that they would insist upon an armistice.' To mitigate such a disaster the Committee recommended the creation of a system of ground defences; but since these could inflict only marginal losses on an attacking force, it advocated also the creation of an air strike force of 20 squadrons—expandable in war time to 50—to retaliate against any aggressor.[149]

Was an attack by the French really so probable as to warrant the expenditure of some £2 million a year on such an insurance policy? The Committee prudently avoided the problem; 'It is for His Majesty's Government,' they suggested, 'to decide as to whether the risk of such attack is sufficiently serious as to necessitate the provision of defences to meet it.'[150] Certainly relations with the French between 1921 and 1923 had reached their lowest point since Fashoda, but it would have been hard to find anyone, inside the Government or outside, who took the eventuality of a French air attack on London very seriously as a possible concomitant even of M. Poincaré's somewhat brusque conduct of foreign affairs. But Mr Balfour quite properly set the issue in the wider context of that nightmare world in which decisions about defence policy inevitably have to be taken. 'A war with France,' he admitted, 'would be a world calamity which seems almost unthinkable; but where national security is concerned even the unthinkable must be faced and we must sometimes assume that to be possible which, in existing circumstances, seems only an evil dream.' If they took no action 'the impossible may after all occur; and . . . even if it does not occur, the mere fear of it may, in quite conceivable circumstances, greatly weaken British diplomacy and may put temptations in the way of French statesmen which they would find it hard to resist.'[151] Even Balfour's far-sighted vision did not encompass the possibility of other powers arising on the Continent with a yet greater capacity for delivering destruction even than France. He does not appear to have had much difficulty in convincing his colleagues, particularly since Winston Churchill, as Chairman of the Economy Committee of the Cabinet, considered that sufficient savings could be made elsewhere in the Service Estimates to find the £2 million needed for the Air Ministry scheme.[152] In August 1922, therefore, the Cabinet approved Air Ministry proposals for the creation of 23 squadrons (14 bomber and 9 fighter); 501 aircraft in all.[153]

The following autumn the Lloyd George coalition disintegrated, and to the incoming Conservative administration even this force looked inadequate. In March 1923 Bonar Law set up a new committee under Lord Salisbury which had the task of examining the relationship between the three Services, the arrangements for coordination of national defence policy, and, not least, 'the standard to be aimed at for defining the strength of the Air Force for purposes of Home and Imperial Defence.'[154] This Committee, with its vast terms of reference, sat until the summer, and ended up by recommending a Home Defence Air Force 52 squadrons strong. Trenchard reiterated his arguments before them in yet stronger terms: 'Air power,' he said, 'holds within itself the possibility of bringing about an early termination of a European War.' But he agreed that, whatever the strength of the Metropolitan Air Force, they could do nothing to protect the population of South-East England against a disaster of unparalleled magnitude. Prompted by Balfour, he admitted that this was 'a position of international unstable equilibrium of the most alarming character'. Balfour himself drew the conclusion that the only ultimate guarantee of peace was 'the certainty of every civilized man, woman and child that everybody will be destroyed if there is a war: everybody and everything.' 'I think perhaps,' he reflected, 'if the energies of our Research Departments in all countries are carried on with sufficient ability, that that might be arrived at.'[155] They were, of course, and it was: the first thermonuclear devices were to be tested only thirty years later.

Nobody questioned, then, the need for a Metropolitan Air Force strong enough, in the words of the Committee's recommendation[156] 'adequately to protect us against air attack by the strongest Air Force within striking distance of this country.' This protection would take the form, not of defence, but of deterrence by the capacity to pose to any aggressor a credible threat of inflicting upon him unacceptable and inescapable destruction. The Army put in a half-hearted claim to control the operations of this force, but in face of the unanimous opposition of the Committee they did not press it.*[157] The Navy, however, gave a great deal

* More valuable was their reiterated reminder that the French Air Force was primarily designed for cooperation with their Army, and that the idea that France, with a revanchist Germany on her flank, might ever get involved in a conflict with Britain, was fantastically improbable. (General Staff Note on French Air Situation, May 1923. ND.31, CAB. 16/47.)

more trouble. They flatly denied that air power would make the slightest difference to war at sea. Fleets even without air cover, they maintained, could protect themselves against air attack; convoys would not be particularly vulnerable from the air; capital ships, whatever American tests might show, could not be sunk from the air; and the ability of the Navy to protect the shores of Britain against invasion was in no way affected.[158] The self-confidence of the Navy was to prove sadly misplaced, but one must remember that their assertions were made at a time when the performance of aircraft was still very limited and their capacity for development entirely unpredictable. Their arguments did not entirely convince the Salisbury Committee, which in its final Report noted the increased vulnerability of shipping within range of land-based aircraft and contemplated the possibility that it might be necessary in time of war to divert shipping from the Channel and the Mediterranean altogether.[159]

The United Kingdom, then, was to be protected primarily by what was already coming to be known as 'deterrence'. But what about the Empire? How was that to be protected, and against whom?

In principle, the situation was still as defined by the Committee of Imperial Defence before the war:

> The maintenance of sea supremacy has been assumed as the basis of the system of Imperial Defence against attack from over the sea. This is the determining factor in shaping the whole defensive policy of the Empire, and is fully recognized by the Admiralty, who have accepted the responsibility of protecting all British territory abroad against organized invasion from the sea.[160]

In practice the position was, as ever, difficult. *Why* it should be difficult was not easy for the layman, in 1919, to see. The German High Seas Fleet was at the bottom of Scapa Flow. The Russians had never re-entered the naval lists after the destruction of their High Seas Fleet by the Japanese in 1904. Armed conflict with France and Italy was highly improbable, and even their combined fleets would offer no serious threat to the Royal Navy. Japan had been a most dutiful ally during the Great War, and even if the Alliance with her was allowed to lapse in 1921, what serious conflict was likely to arise with that friendly and co-operative government? As for the United States, she seemed set on building at least to parity with the Royal Navy for much the same reasons as Germany had before the war—'for the necessary purposes of her greatness'; but the prudent avoidance of armed conflict with the United States had been a tacit principle of British policy since the beginning of the century. And would not the League of Nations in future preserve peace? What, in fact, was the Royal Navy now for?

The Admiralty knew. It was to protect the communications and territories of the Empire in a world in which no combinations were permanent and no events foreseeable—a view which the governments of Australia and New Zealand most enthusiastically shared. The United States might never be an enemy, but they might again be neutral in a conflict in which Britain was attacking her adversary's trade, and a pretty hostile neutral at that. Certainly the U.S. Navy did not rule out a conflict with Britain as a possible contingency: some of its senior officers indeed, seem to have looked forward to it with a certain relish.[161] As for Japan, her imperial ambitions might not always be confined to the mainland of Asia; her connection with Indian nationalist agitation was suspected even if it could not be proved; and the attack on Port Arthur in 1904 had shown that when she did strike, she did so unexpectedly and fast. The German danger had forced the Royal Navy to abandon the Pacific to Japan's discretion, but that danger had been eliminated. Financial stringency made it impossible to maintain a fleet of sufficient size simultaneously to protect the United Kingdom and to defend her Eastern Empire against possible attack by a major naval power. It was essential, therefore, that a base should be provided in the Far East from which the Fleet could operate, and which could defend itself during the six weeks that it might take for the Fleet to get out there. As the site for this base the Admiralty, in spring 1921, recommended the island of Singapore; a proposal which, although it involved an expenditure of nearly £5 m, was approved by the Committee of Imperial Defence and the Cabinet within a matter of weeks, and announced as a *fait accompli* to the Imperial Conference which met the following June.[162]

In so far as the decision implied the abandonment of the Japanese alliance, it was greeted with little enthusiasm by the Australians, and there were many voices to suggest that by alienating the Japanese the building of the base would bring into being the very threat it was created to avert. But Australian doubts were countered by the strong Canadian argument that the continuation of the alliance would make any serious accommodation with the United States impossible, and the Cabinet with some reluctance accepted this view. The result has been well summed up by Max Beloff: 'Instead of the Anglo-Japanese Alliance, based on a nice calculation of mutual interests and relative capacities, Britain was to enter into a new system whose functioning would principally depend upon the incalculable shifts and whims of American democracy.'[163]

It was a decision that some influential Englishmen were later to regret. Only 'if we can emancipate ourselves from thraldom to the United States,' wrote Sir Warren Fisher, Permanent Under-Secretary to the Treasury in 1934, 'and thus free ourselves to establish durable relations with Japan [can we] concentrate on the paramount danger at our very threshold.'[164] Certainly British historians can take very little pleasure in remarking that this was probably the first time since the reign of Charles II that Britain had adjusted her foreign policy in order to conciliate a more powerful nation than herself. But the government at the time had good reason to suppose that they had no alternative if they wished to preserve at least naval parity with the United States. It can be argued that however great its naval power, United States policy was never likely to pose so serious a military danger to the British Empire as was that of a disgruntled and ruthless Japan, so priority should have gone to conciliating the latter. On the other hand, if there ever was to be a conflict in the Pacific, Japan could never be so effective an ally as the United States. The balance of probabilities was delicate, and it is doubtful whether the decision was taken on grounds of power politics alone.

In any case all such probabilities, at the time of the Washington Conference, appeared hypothetical to the point of fantasy, and remained so until the end of the decade. It is not surprising that the Labour Government in March 1924, declaring its intention of establishing conditions of international confidence which would make disarmament possible, should have abandoned work on the Singapore Base on the grounds that it would 'hamper the establishment of this confidence and lay our good faith open to suspicion;'[165] a decision greeted by no less an expert than Smuts as 'a bold move towards enduring peace'. Nor is it surprising that, when the Baldwin Government reversed that decision on returning to office the following autumn, progress on the base was lethargic and delayed by continual inter-service controversy. The Foreign Secretary, Austen Chamberlain, told his colleagues in January 1925 that he regarded 'the prospect of war in the Far East as very remote'. On the strength of his assurances the Committee of Imperial Defence agreed that 'in existing circumstances aggressive action against the British Empire on the part of Japan within the next ten years is not a contingency seriously to be apprehended.'[166]

Even this did not satisfy the Chancellor of the Exchequer, Winston Churchill; who having spent five years at the Admiralty building up the Royal Navy was now spending another five at the Treasury trying with equal zest to cut it down again. He urged the Prime Minister to tell the Admiralty 'that they are not expected to be in a position to encounter Japan in the Pacific Ocean and they are not to prepare for such a contingency. . . . They should be made to recast all their plans and scales and standards on the basis that no naval war against a first-class Navy is likely to take place in the next twenty years.' In this he was fortunately not successful; but he did persuade the Committee of Imperial Defence, in July 1928, to lay it down 'as a standing assumption that at any given date there will be no major war for ten years from that date; and that this should rule unless or until, on the initiative of the Foreign Office or one of the fighting Services or otherwise, it is decided to alter it.'[167]

This was the famous, or notorious, Ten Year Rule in its final form. But it was accepted only subject to annual review and to its being 'the duty of any Department and the right of any Dominion Government to ask for it to be reconsidered at any time.' Since it was anyway abandoned within four years, the real damage that it did to the defensive capabilities of the British Empire may have been less than has been generally supposed.

In spite of all that Mr Churchill could do to prevent it, the Navy continued to prepare doggedly for a war with Japan, as the Royal Air Force continued to prepare doggedly for a war with France. The Army showed little interest in either. In so far as it visualized a conflict with any major power it had in mind yet a third adversary: the Soviet Union.

This was natural enough. With no immediate problems to face in Europe, and with the gradual revival of Russian power, the Army's main military problem seemed once again to be the defence of India. Within a few years of the end of the war British and Russian agents had settled down again to the Great Game throughout Asia which had been temporarily interrupted in 1907. The Foreign Office shared the fears of the Army. In 1926 Austen Chamberlain informed his ministerial colleagues that in the opinion of the Foreign Office 'the greatest danger at the present time was that which emanated from Russia and which took the form of constant anti-British activities wherever opportunities occurred of rousing or increasing anti-British feelings... Our policy [he concluded] should be based on the assumption that Russia is the enemy and not Japan.'[168] The following spring the Chief of the Imperial General Staff, Sir George Milne, defined the problem more precisely. Russia, he wrote, was 'pursuing a consistent policy whose aim is ultimately to undermine British supremacy in India. Added to this we have an unstable Government in Afghanistan whose ruler is pursuing the traditional policy of playing off the British against the Russians... A further factor in the problem is that of the semi-independent tribes on our North-West Frontier. . . . Finally we have to consider the internal conditions of India;' conditions which two years later in 1929 were to erupt in widespread communal disturbances and revolt. The change in régime in Russia, 'marks the start of a new era in Russian methods but not in policy.' She was now practising such effective techniques of subversion that 'it is unlikely, indeed it is unnecessary, that Russia should move a single soldier across the Oxus before...further extension of her territories takes place.'[169]

Once again Afghanistan appeared the weak point in British India's defences, and a Committee of Imperial Defence Sub-Committee which sat throughout 1927 reported at the end of that year in the same sense as had Lord Morley's Committee twenty years earlier. 'By our own plain interest,' it stated, 'our obligations to guard the independence and integrity of Afghanistan are unimpaired.'[170] The Government of India, it agreed, could not be expected to bear the charge of a major war to defend Afghanistan against the Soviet Union. The War Office therefore worked out a plan for a campaign 'based on the principles of simplicity, celerity and audacity' requiring from England only some 11 divisions, or a quarter of a million men. This, it was hoped, need not involve conscription: such an army, the committee concluded a shade optimistically, could probably be raised on a voluntary basis.[171]

But the true problem of Indian defence now lay deeper than this. India's participation in the Great War, while in appearance, like that of the white Dominions, bearing witness to the power of the British Empire, in practice went far to undermine it. On the one hand it conclusively strengthened the hand of those in England who wished to set India on the path to Home Rule; and from the Montagu-Chelmsford reforms the British government could only go forward at a speed which, however great they made it, could never quite keep up with Indian demands. On the other, to quote the unkind but penetrating words of Mr Pannikar, 'the Indian soldier who fought on the Marne came back to India with other ideas of the Sahib than those he was taught to believe by years of propaganda.'[172] In 1923 the General Staff reported 'sedition and disloyalty in the Indian Army amounting almost to mutiny'.[173] The Government and High Command in India repeatedly warned London that they could not guarantee, in the event of emergencies, the internal situation in India permitting them to despatch Indian troops overseas for general purposes of Imperial defence; and when in 1927 the process of 'Indianization' of the Indian Army began, the War Office considered that this exposed the force to 'the risk of a progressive deterioration in the standard of efficiency, without any corresponding economy,' and that 'it would not be safe, at any rate until the experiment had proved successful, to rely either in actual warfare or even for the maintenance of law and order, on units in which the British element is within sight of disappearing.'[174] So far from being an asset, India looked like becoming the heaviest liability of all.

In 1929 India erupted in a series of internal upheavals and frontier disturbances which were to keep the British forces there pinned down in peacekeeping operations for about three years. And India was not the only place where this occurred. In the Middle East nationalist agitation was no less strong and the imperial presence no less resented; but after the initial rebellions in Egypt and Mesopotamia the British had been able to establish relations with the local régimes which made unnecessary the employment of any military force other than the remarkably economical and effective air-policing operations, in Iraq, Transjordan and later Aden, of the Royal Air Force. Britain's huge new responsibilities in the area in fact gave surprisingly little trouble, and her presence there, as Elizabeth Monroe has put it, 'brought it the kind of economic gain which, while breeding no gratitude, produces a grumbling tranquillity.'[175] Thus it might have continued but for the fatal embarrassment of Palestine, where in 1929 the revolt of the native population against the Jewish immigrants, long simmering, broke out with a violence far beyond the capacity of the Royal Air Force to contain. A military garrison had to be established which thereafter was involved in endless and hopeless policing tasks to which the Second World War provided an almost welcome, though, alas, temporary relief. The Palestine ulcer was gradually to poison Britain's position throughout the entire Middle East. As a result of it her relations with Iraq, Egypt, and even Transjordan deteriorated, until by 1939, to quote Miss Monroe again, 'Middle Eastern society as a whole was simmering beneath a crust consisting of British military power and royal conservatism.'[176]

These activities, together with protective duties in that Alsatia of the international capitalist system, China, occupied the British Army quite as fully as had its comparable imperial policing duties before the General Staff had begun to play its European War Games in 1905. The regular soldiers returned to these traditional occupations with little sign of regret. The vast corpus of experience of fighting in Europe was allowed to melt away: not until 1932 was a Committee set up to study the lessons of the First World War. Experiments with armoured warfare were taken up half-heartedly and abandoned with little reluctance. Yet in 1925, by the Locarno Treaties, Britain assumed in Europe military obligations far more precise than any that had bound her before 1914. These obligations, to guarantee the German–Belgian and German–French frontiers against aggression from either side—to say nothing of maintaining the demilitarized status of the Rhineland—were discussed with and approved by the

Chiefs of Staff; who expressed in particular their satisfaction that so large an area beyond the Channel should be neutralized as a possible base for air attacks on the United Kingdom. 'For us,' the CIGS, Sir George Milne, told the Cabinet, in a phrase which Mr Baldwin was one day to make better known, 'it is only incidentally a question of French security; essentially it is a matter of British security. . . . The true strategic position of Great Britain is on the Rhine.'[177]

The following year, 1926, the Foreign Office reminded the Chiefs of Staff of the general obligations Britain had assumed under the Covenant of the League in general and of the Locarno guarantees in particular and suggested, very firmly, that 'The more the nations of Europe become convinced of our readiness to fulfil our guarantee, the less likelihood will there be that we shall be called upon to do so.'[178] To this the Chiefs of Staff replied with a brutally frank statement of their own list of priorities which was markedly at variance with that of the Foreign Office.

The size of the forces of the Crown maintained by Great Britain is governed by various conditions peculiar to each service, and is not arrived at by any calculations of the requirements of foreign policy, nor is it possible that they ever should be so calculated. Thus, though the Expeditionary Force, together with a limited number of Air Force Squadrons, constitute the only military instrument available for immediate use in Europe or elsewhere outside Imperial territory in support of foreign policy, they are so available only when the requirements of Imperial Defence so permit.

It follows that so far as commitments on the Continent are concerned, the Services can only take note of them . . .[179]

This remarkable declaration of military independence

seemed to cause little concern in Whitehall; any more than did repeated reminders by the Chiefs of Staff that they had no plans for implementing the Locarno guarantees and had received no instructions to make any.[180] The Expeditionary Force to which the Chiefs of Staff referred consisted of two skeletal divisions made up of units temporarily without other employment; and the world situation ensured that these did not remain without other employment for long. In 1925, in fact, as in 1900, Britain's imperial responsibilities rendered her impotent to bring serious influence to bear on those developments in Europe on which her security ultimately depended.

Moreover in assuming obligations under the Locarno Treaties, Britain assumed them alone. An optional clause in the agreements provided for the Dominions to join in if they so wished, but they very clearly did not so wish. Smuts opposed the Treaties, as we have seen, 'almost to the last ditch', and so did the Government of Canada.[181] At the Imperial Conference of 1926 the Dominions passed a resolution congratulating the British Government on 'its share in this successful contribution towards the promotion of the peace of the world'.[182] But their private comments were less laudatory. 'For the first time since the Great War,' one Canadian historian has written, 'a British Government had asserted the national interest of the United Kingdom against the interest of imperial concern'.[183] If the Foreign Office was alarmed at guarantees which could not in the event be fulfilled, the Dominions were still more alarmed at Britain giving any guarantees at all. Still, the League, the Covenant, and General Disarmament might make all these fears and promises unnecessary. Time alone could show.

5 Limited Liability, 1932–1938

On 2nd February 1932 the Disarmament Conference for which the world had been preparing for the past five years met in Geneva. The omens were not favourable. The economic recovery which had made possible the growing confidence and the increasing international cooperation of the Locarno Era had ended three years earlier in disastrous collapse. In Germany, statesmen whose ability to conduct a moderate foreign policy depended on their success in maintaining domestic prosperity were being driven from the scene by parties of the right and left which practised violence at home and advocated it abroad. In the Far East, the stiffening resistance of the Chinese to foreign exploitation presented the Japanese with problems which their soldiers on the spot were anyhow inclined to solve by force; and their civilian rulers, grappling with intractable economic problems at home, had little power and perhaps little will to restrain them. For those who believed that the Covenant of the League of Nations had ushered in a new era in world history based on rational cooperation and collective security—and these comprised the most articulate part, if not a majority, of the British electorate—the Disarmament Conference represented the last, best hope of mankind. To others—including the Chiefs of Staff—it was a pious irrelevance. Even if collective security was a workable concept it required arms in the last resort to enforce it, and Britain for one had no arms to enforce it with.

On 4th February, two days after the Conference began, the British Ambassador telegraphed from Tokyo: 'Tension here is so great that a false step might cause the Japanese to take some action which would render war with the Powers almost inevitable.'[184] If war did come, the Royal Navy had only light forces in the Far East. Its bases at Hong Kong and Singapore were for all practical purposes indefensible. 'The whole of our territory in the Far East,' reported the Chiefs of Staff to the Committee of Imperial Defence in their Annual Review of Imperial Defence Policy the same month, 'as well as the coastline of India and the Dominions and our vast trade and shipping, lies open to attack. . . . What the political reaction in India and the various colonies would be,' they added grimly, 'we leave it to the experts to determine.' And they quoted a further message from the Ambassador in Tokyo, to the effect that cooperation with Japan 'may well entail further fewer military commitments than thwarting her.'[185]

This diplomatic circumlocution could have been expressed more pithily: 'If you can't lick 'em, join 'em.' It was advice which some British statesmen were to find increasingly attractive as the decade ran its depressing course. Perhaps it was more realistic than that given by the League of Nations Union, that Britain should convoke the Assembly of the League and apply in the Far East whatever pressure of a diplomatic and military character might be necessary to re-establish peace. 'It must be apparent to any well-informed person,' commented the Chiefs of Staff on this resolution, 'that such action might result in a resort to force by Japan, and that the brunt of a war must fall on the British Empire.'[186]

So within a few days of the opening of the Disarmament Conference the Chiefs of Staff were formally recommending that the Ten Year Rule should be cancelled and that 'a start should be made in providing for commitments that are purely defensive, including the defence of Bases.'[187] To this the Treasury did not formally object: the Rule, they said, had not been 'an essay in prophecy, but a working hypothesis intended to relieve the Chiefs of Staff from the responsibility of preparing against contingencies which the Government believe to be either remote or beyond the financial capacity of the country to provide against.' But they pointed out unanswerably 'that in present circumstances we are no more in a position financially and economically to engage in a major war in the Far East than we are militarily.' Barely six months had passed since Britain had been forced off the Gold Standard. The country's debts were enormous. What was needed, above all, they insisted, was a 'period of recuperation, diminishing taxes, increased trade and employment'. The Treasury therefore submitted 'that today's financial and economic risks are far the most serious and urgent that the country has to face.'[188]

In the circumstances of the time, the arguments of the Chiefs of Staff and of the Treasury seemed equally convincing. On 23rd March therefore the Cabinet cancelled the Ten Year Rule but warned 'that this must not be taken to justify an expanding expenditure by the Defence Services without regard to the very serious financial and economic situation which still obtains.'[189] An increase of £5 million in defence expenditure was thus possible in 1933; but since this did no more than restore the 1931 level of £107 m. (the 1932 expenditure of £183 million had been the lowest since the war) it did not go far to fill the gaps of which the Chiefs of Staff had long been too uncomfortably aware.

1932 set a pattern which was to change little over the next six years. Financial stringency forced a Treasury which, although it had heard of John Maynard Keynes, had little reason to love him, to impose on the Services such restrictions that one angry senior officer complained that the Government seemed less concerned to set the national defences in order than to have enough money to pay an indemnity to a victorious enemy after the war had been lost.[190] Public opinion regarded the prospect of another war with dread, and found it easy to believe that rearmament was more likely to hasten than to avert it. The Labour and Liberal Parties continued to pin their faith on 'collective security' which, they believed, would make rearmament unnecessary. The Conservative Party, while supporting rearmament, urged a policy of 'no continental entanglements' which made the development of an appropriate defence policy and of the arms to maintain it almost equally difficult. The Cabinets of MacDonald and Baldwin showed in their conduct of foreign policy an anxious attention to electoral moods which would have gladdened the heart of E. D. Morel and his colleagues in the Union of Democratic Control; moods which they personally profoundly shared. The Cabinets which governed Britain in the 1930s were composed of men who believed that almost no price was too high to pay to avoid another war. The exceptions, curiously enough, were those who had had first-hand experience of war, Anthony Eden and Alfred Duff Cooper; who knew that, vile as the experience was, it was not utterly intolerable, and there might be others yet worse.

These moods were also shared, as we have seen, in the Dominions; in Canada and South Africa out of isolationist sentiment, in Australia because of a threat very much nearer home, while New Zealand bravely upheld the flag of the League of Nations and collective security till the bitter end. When German troops reentered the demilitarized Rhineland in 1936, Canada and South Africa made clear their total hostility to any Franco–British attempt to carry out their guarantees under the Locarno Treaties. At the Imperial Conference in 1937 the Dominions issued a ringing declaration in favour of appeasement. 'Differences of political creed,' they declared, 'should be no obstacle to friendly relations between Governments and countries. . . . Nothing would be more damaging to the hopes of international appeasement than the division, real or apparent, of the world into opposing groups.'[191] And in March 1938, when the Czechoslovak problem began to darken the political horizon, Mr Malcolm MacDonald, the Dominions Secretary, said that the issue was one on which the Commonwealth might well 'break in pieces'. South Africa and Canada he said, would not fight 'to prevent certain Germans rejoining their Fatherland.'[192] It was even less likely that they would fight to uphold that archaic and discredited doctrine, the Balance of Power.

So the Empire brought Britain no strength in her dealings with Germany. Yet British strength had nevertheless to be dissipated in the Empire's defence. In the minds of the Government's two most influential military advisers during this period, the Chairman of the Chiefs of Staff Committee, Admiral Sir Ernle Chatfield, and the Secretary of the Cabinet and of the Committee of Imperial Defence, Sir Maurice Hankey, the need to defend Britain's Eastern Empire bulked at least as large as the need to redress the balance of force in Europe, and at times, one is tempted to believe, very much larger.

In view of the growing power, ambition and bellicosity of Japan this was understandable enough. Britain's commitment to the defence of Australia and New Zealand was, after all, absolute. It was spelled out again for the Australian Government by the Chiefs of Staff in the summer of 1932. The security of the Empire, they reminded the Australians, depended on the Royal Navy maintaining a capital fleet of adequate strength which provided cover by concentrating against the enemy fleet. Since this could not prevent commerce raiding by enemy units, cruiser squadrons would be necessary as well; as would be land forces to guard against minor raids. The individual parts of the Empire were encouraged to contribute to the former and provide the latter. Since the main fleet could not concentrate immediately at the point of greatest danger, there would be a 'period before relief' for which the various component parts of the Empire would have to provide on their own. 'Provided that the British Fleet arrives in time and finds a properly equipped base at Singapore,' the Chiefs of Staff concluded reassuringly, 'Australia has nothing to fear beyond a sporadic attack.' But if it did not, they warned, then 'Australian interests become exposed to attack on a considerable scale.'[193]

The Singapore base was perhaps the easiest requirement to provide, and permission for the long delayed and frequently interrupted work to proceed was given by the Cabinet in June 1932. The Committee of Imperial Defence suggested that 'there would be no necessity for a specific announcement that it was now proposed to proceed with the defences of Singapore, though it was recognized that questions might be asked in Parliament.'[194] But would there be a British Fleet available to go there? The entire Singapore strategy assumed that no major naval threat was likely to arise in Europe, and in the 1920s the assumption seemed reasonable enough. In the 1930s it grew rapidly less plausible. It was the vital need to maintain a favourable naval balance in Europe that led the Admiralty into negotiating the Anglo-German Naval Agreement in June 1935, by which the Germans agreed to build only up to 35 per cent of the British strength in capital ships; an agreement which tore a great rift in the Stresa Front which had been cobbled together with France and Italy only two months earlier. Further, the desire to maintain this agreement was to make the Admiralty reluctant to conduct naval staff conversations with France concerning possible hostilities in the Mediterranean.[195] The requirements of Imperial Defence, in fact, ran counter to any such continental entanglements. 'The broad principles on which our Empire strategy has always been based should not be forgotten,' declared the Chiefs of Staff when the possibility of staff conversations was mooted in 1936, 'nor should the lessons of history be overlooked. The greater our commitments to Europe, the less will be our ability to secure our Empire and its communications.'[196]

But by 1936 the Royal Navy had already got itself into a totally unexpected commitment in Europe from which it was determined to shake itself free. Before 1935 Italy had not been reckoned as one of Britain's potential enemies: two years earlier indeed the Committee for Imperial Defence had explicitly recommended that she should, together with France and the United States, be left out of calculation altogether; and as late as the spring of 1935 the Chiefs of Staff in their Annual Review mentioned Britain's Mediterranean commitments only in an Appendix listing her general obligations overseas.[197] The Abyssinian crisis in the autumn changed all that. When war with Italy to enforce the League's sanctions appeared a possibility, the Mediterranean Fleet looked forward with some enthusiasm to fighting an enemy for whom they had never had much respect and who was strategically vulnerable. But from Whitehall the view was different. 'I have mixed feelings about the war . . .,' wrote Chatfield; 'A hostile Italy is a real menace to our

Imperial communications and defence system. We have relied on practically abandoning the Mediterranean if we send
the Fleet East.'[198] The Chiefs of Staff warned the Government against even a victorious war with Italy: 'In a single-
handed war especially we might suffer considerable exhaus-
tion and our resources for fulfilling our wider responsibilities
might be impaired.'[199] There was in fact to be no war; but
the military and naval commitments consequent on the
Abyssinian crisis paralysed the British armed forces when, in
March 1936, Hitler reoccupied the Rhineland. A war with
Germany, the Chiefs of Staff then warned the Cabinet,
would be 'a disaster for which the Services with their existing commitments in the Mediterranean are totally unprepared.'[200] The following June they were urging the end of
sanctions against Italy. 'Our interests lie in a peaceful
Mediterranean,' they advised, 'and this can only be achieved
by returning to a state of friendly relations with Italy.'[201]
Imperial Defence, in short, required peace, and hence appeasement, in Europe. Four-square behind Mr Chamberlain when in 1937 he began his search for friendship with
at least one of the dictators, stood the Chairman of the
Chief of Staffs Committee and the Secretary of the Committee for Imperial Defence: both staunch believers in
Britain's traditional strategy.

The Navy's attitude towards a Continental involvement was
thus very much what it had been before 1914, and now with
very much better reason. To understand the position of the
Army and the Royal Air Force, we must retrace our steps
to October 1933. In that month Germany walked out, both
of the Disarmament Conference and of the League of
Nations—which Japan had left the previous March. John
Wilmot won that notorious by-election in East Fulham
which had so considerable an effect on Baldwin;[202] and—for

our purposes more important than either of these—the Chiefs
of Staff produced an Annual Review which stated, among
other things, that 'Germany is not only starting to rearm,
but . . . she will continue this process until within a few
years hence she will again have to be reckoned as a formidable military power.' As soon as she felt strong enough, the
Review continued, she would 'attain her ends in a war of
offence in the East, combined if necessary with a defensive
in the West. It would therefore seem that at any time within
the next, say, three to five years we may be faced with demands for military intervention on the Continent, either as a
result of repercussions arising out of attempts to prevent
German rearmament by means of threats or sanctions, or in
order to implement our obligations to provide assistance in
case of aggression by Germany under the Covenant of the
League or the Locarno Treaties.'[203]

To fulfil these European obligations, the Chiefs of Staff
pointed out, the British Army could provide at most two
divisions, which could not be reinforced for many months;
and 'one of the great lessons of the last war,' they warned,
'is that it is impossible to limit the liability once we are committed to any theatre of operations.' Anyhow, war in Europe
would certainly mean trouble elsewhere which would make
competing demands on Britain's military resources. 'In fact,'
the Review concluded, 'we are forced to the conclusion that,
should war break out in Europe, far from our having the
means to intervene, we should be able to do little more than
hold the frontiers and outposts of the Empire during the first
few months of the war.'

This statement sufficiently alarmed even the Chancellor
of the Exchequer, Neville Chamberlain, into admitting that
the financial dangers facing the country were no longer
worse than the military.[204] The Committee of Imperial

Defence set up a Sub-Committee under Hankey's Chairmanship, consisting of the Chiefs of Staff and the Permanent Under-Secretaries of the Foreign Office and the Treasury, Sir Robert Vansittart and Sir Warren Fisher, to prepare a programme for meeting the worst deficiencies in the Armed Services. This was the Defence Requirements Committee. Since the report which it submitted the following February was to provide the basis for Britain's defence policy during the ensuing five years, it is worth spending a few moments examining its proceedings.[205]

These were clearly dominated by the civilians. Vansittart and Fisher between them made short work of Chatfield's and Hankey's contention that Japan was the major adversary that Britain had to face. The base at Singapore must certainly be completed, they agreed, but all policy should be based on reestablishing friendly relations with Japan even at cost of offending the United States. 'We cannot,' the final Report stated, 'overstate the importance we attach to getting back, not to an alliance (since that would not be practical politics) but at least to our old terms of cordiality and mutual respect with Japan.' Germany, on the other hand, was 'the ultimate potential enemy against whom all our "long range" defence policy must be directed;' and this was primarily a matter for the Army and the Royal Air Force.[206] The Chief of the Imperial General Staff, General Sir Archibald Montgomery-Massingberd, stoutly asserted that the strongest Expeditionary Force that the Army could find was one of four infantry divisions, a cavalry division and a tank brigade. Any reinforcements would have to come from the Territorial Army; but to bring the Territorials up to operational standard would, he said, 'entail expenditure in peace that is beyond our means.'[207] In vain Fisher and Vansittart urged him to name the size of the Army he really wanted and leave it to others to scale it down. To do so, he insisted, 'would unbalance the Report as between various items and as between three Services. He was of the opinion that the expenditure of £250,000 a year would be sufficient to give great encouragement to the Territorials.' So it was left at that. There was no suggestion that a force even larger than five regular and fourteen Territorial Divisions might one day be needed, and that preliminary preparations should be undertaken to create one. Never Again.

The same modesty was shown by the Royal Air Force, which asked only that the original programme approved in 1923 for 52 squadrons for Home Defence should be completed. Vansittart and Fisher however pointed out that that programme had been planned only to protect London and South-East England against attack by France. Was it enough also to defend the Midlands and the North against an attack by Germany? No, admitted the Chief of Air Staff, Sir Edward Ellington, it was not. That would require another 25 squadrons and he had no idea what that would cost. 'The matter would have to be treated as an emergency and special powers provided.' And, interposed the Chief of the Imperial General Staff, it would unbalance the Defence Estimates as between the three Services.[208]

Starved of resources for years, uncertain of their ability to recruit the necessary manpower and conscious of the lack of any armaments-base to make major expansion possible, the timidity of the Service Chiefs, pathetic as it now appears, is understandable. In the case of the Army, indeed, it was doubtful whether the Government could be persuaded to sanction any Expeditionary Force at all. Hankey warned the Defence Requirements Committee that 'it would be essential to include in the Committee's report a clearly-worded statement as to why it was considered necessary to organize an

Expeditionary Force to fight in a possible continental war;' and he was right.[209] It was on this issue that Ministers fastened when they came to consider the Report in May 1934. The justification given in the Report for sending a force to the Continent was that 'if the Low Countries were in the hands of a hostile power, not only would the frequency and intensity of air attack in London be increased, but the whole of the industrial areas of the Midlands and North of England would be brought within the area of penetration of hostile air attacks.' This was brushed aside. Mr Chamberlain dismissed it on the grounds that if the Belgian frontier was properly fortified the Germans could not get through, and if it was not the British forces would arrive too late anyway. 'It seemed to him,' he said, echoing consciously or unconsciously the ideas being propagated by the Defence Correspondent of *The Times*, Captain Liddell Hart,[210] 'that our experience in the last war indicated that we ought to put our major resources into our Navy and our Air Force . . . the Army must be maintained, so that it can be used in other parts of the world'; while J. H. Thomas, who spoke with the authentic accent of the common man, said flatly that whatever the Chiefs of Staff might say, 'it would be necessary to convince public opinion of the necessity of sending an expeditionary force to the Continent.'[211] Never Again.

So the Chiefs of Staff provided another strongly argued paper, restating not only the military, naval and air arguments for sending land forces to protect the Low Countries but the political consequences of failing to do so. These came near to stating again the basic principles of the Balance of Power:

No one can doubt our necessity for a strong Navy and Air Force. Nevertheless, unless we possess some land forces capable of early intervention on the Continent of Europe potential enemies as well as potential allies will probably consider . . . our power to influence a decision by arms inadequate. The influence which this may have on international policy and the cause of peace may be far-reaching in the extreme. . . . It is not so much the size of the forces we can send as the moral effect which their arrival would have on Belgian defence, and the knowledge that behind those forces is the whole might of the British Empire ready and determined to wage war with all its available resources in defence of the independence of the peoples whose frontiers we have guaranteed. . . . Quite apart from any question of implementing our guarantees under the various Pacts and Covenants which we have signed, the security of this country demands that we should be prepared to fight for the integrity of Belgium and Holland.[212]

These arguments impressed at least Baldwin, but like Thomas he wondered how far they would impress the British public. 'At present,' he suggested, on 11 June 1934, 'the public were not in the least familiar with the position and he thought it was time they were made aware what the position really was. From an air point of view, our frontiers had been moved from Dover to the Rhine. When these fundamental things had been explained to the people and they understood, it might be possible to lead them on.'[213]

They certainly did not impress Chamberlain in his role as Chancellor of the Exchequer, who submitted a paper of his own on the subject.[214] The proposals of the Defence Requirements Committee involved additional expenditure, over five years, of some £97 m.; not excessive for the tasks they had outlined, he agreed, but none the less 'impossible to carry out'. They could be financed only by a special loan and that, he declared, was 'the broad road that leads to destruction'. Even if no public mention was made of an Expeditionary

Force, he considered 'expenditure on the Army ... bulks so large in the total as to give rise to the most alarmist ideas of future intentions and commitments.' In their programme, he suggested, the Government should instead give overriding priority to the measures which the public would understand and approve—those directly related to the defence of the United Kingdom; and 'our best defence,' he considered, 'would be the existence of a deterrent force so powerful as to render success in attack too doubtful to be worthwhile. I submit that this is most likely to be attained by the establishment of an Air Force based on this country of a size and efficiency calculated to inspire respect in the mind of a possible enemy.' Only if deterrence failed should they consider measures for actual defence: anti-aircraft, fighter squadrons and 'finally, the conversion of the Army into an effectively-equipped force capable of operating with Allies in holding the Low Countries.' So instead of the 52 squadrons asked for by the Royal Air Force, they should provide 80. Instead of the £40 m. recommended for the Army they should provide £19 m. As for the Royal Navy, suggested Chamberlain, the whole idea of sending the fleet to Singapore should be scrapped. Singapore should be kept as a base for light craft only, and the rapprochement with Japan urged by Vansittart and Fisher should be vigorously pursued. All this would reduce expenditure by about a third, to the manageable figure of £59 m.

Mr Chamberlain's suggestions were at least coherent; but they were not popular with his colleagues of the Service Ministries.[215] The proposal virtually to abandon Singapore appalled the Navy. Lord Hailsham for the War Office pointed out that the air deterrent would be of little value without the forward bases in Belgium and without the ground defences in Britain which the Army would have to provide. Lord Londonderry for the Air Ministry said he regarded the Chancellor's proposals as being 'better designed for public consumption than for real utility', ignoring as they did the whole question of reserve capacity to sustain a prolonged campaign. But Mr Chamberlain carried the bulk of the Cabinet with him. His proposals to abandon the Far East, it is true were more than even MacDonald was prepared to accept. But Baldwin agreed that expansion of the Royal Air Force 'was regarded by members of the Cabinet as something in the nature of a gesture to Europe and especially to Germany [and that] from the political point of view it was necessary to do something to satisfy the semi-panic conditions which existed now about the air.' As for the Army even the Secretary of State for War agreed that 'it would be a big mistake to make any declaration . . . at the present time. A good deal of education was required and to come out with the whole programme now would have a very alarming effect on opinion generally.'[216]

So the Army cuts were accepted. A modified Air Ministry plan, for building the Metropolitan Air Force up to 84 squadrons, was accepted; and this was the only part of the programme which Mr Baldwin felt it prudent to announce to Parliament on 30th July 1934, when he began his cautious programme of public education in the facts of political life by reminding his audience 'When you think of the defence of England you no longer think of the chalk cliffs of Dover; you think of the Rhine. That is where our frontier lies.'[217]

Deterrence theory had not yet reached the degree of sophistication to which American analysts were to take it when, twenty years later, under very comparable circumstances, the United States Government adopted a precisely similar policy in order to obtain maximum effectiveness at least cost. But even in the 1930s it was apparent that a deterrent is not credible if the adversary possesses a more powerful capacity to deter you from using it. *Vis-à-vis* Germany, Britain was at a serious disadvantage in the conduct of air war. British targets were concentrated and within easy reach, German targets were diffused over a wide geographical area. The same weight of bombs, ferried over the same distance, could do far more effective damage to the British economy, and probably British morale as well, than it could to the German. In 1934 the Air Staff calculated that with a first-line force of 1,230 aircraft Germany could drop 75 tons a day on England from German territory, and 150 tons if she occupied the Low Countries. Casualties they estimated at 50 per ton.[218] These estimates rose rapidly in step with British intelligence of German air strength. By 1936 the official estimate was 600 tons, with casualties during the first week of the war at 150,000. By 1939 it was 700 tons; with perhaps a 'knock-out blow' of 3,500 tons in the first 24 hours.*[219]

As against this, what could the Royal Air Force do, even if the Government fulfilled the pledge given in the House of Commons by Mr Baldwin in March 1934, that 'in air strength and in air power this country shall no longer be in a position inferior to any country within striking distance of these shores?'[220] It remains one of the most remarkable facts in the whole history of British defence policy that the Royal Air Force, which since 1918 had based its entire strategic doctrine and its *raison d'être* on the vital part which strategic

* In fact the heaviest air raid on Britain in the Second World War was that on London on 19 April 1941, when the Luftwaffe dropped 1,026 tons of high explosive. 500 tons were dropped on Coventry on 14th November 1940. Otherwise the weight of attack fluctuated between 400 and 50 tons of high explosive per raid. (Basil Collier: *The Defence of the United Kingdom*, London 1957, Appendix XXX.)

bombing would play in future wars, had before 1937 carried out no studies as to how this was actually to be done. 'Our belief in the bomber was intuitive,' confessed Marshal of the Royal Air Force Sir John Slessor in his memoirs—'a matter of faith.'[221] The studies which it did carry out in 1937 quickly revealed, in the words of their official historians 'that there was no clear idea what was operationally possible, what targets could be reached, how far they could be hit, what would happen to them if they were hit, or what were likely to be the casualties incurred.'[222] As a result of these studies the Air Staff recommended that British bombing should be directed in a counter-force role against German air force targets to reduce German striking power, rather than against German civilian industrial targets as had previously been intended. It was 'unsafe to assume,' they reported, 'that under our present programme our air force, even with the cooperation of the French, will be able by attacking the morale of the German people to produce an effect in any way comparable with that which would result from a German attack on our own.' But even this counter-force strategy, they concluded gloomily, 'could be no more than a palliative holding out no hope of eventual victory, even if it could avoid defeat.'[223] In November 1938 the Commander in Chief of Bomber Command was asserting that *any* operations involving deep penetration into Germany, irrespective of target, might end in major disaster; and when war broke out in September 1939 Bomber Command thought it prudent to confine its activities to attacks on the German Fleet and to the dropping of propaganda leaflets over Germany. So far from providing any kind of a deterrent, the Royal Air Force found itself most effectively deterred.

The story has already been told, in the official histories, of the successive aircraft construction programmes between 1934 and 1939 which constantly lagged, as in some bad dream, behind the German achievement.[224] Here we need only point out that at no stage in this period did British air strength, existing or prospective, appear to have had the slightest influence on Hitler's policy or indeed on that of anyone else. 1935 saw Germany's denunciation of the Versailles limitations on her armed forces and Italy's open alignment with the revisionist powers. Deterrence was clearly not enough. In July the Defence Requirements Committee was reassembled and invited to produce a new programme in the light of the worsening international situation.

The report the Committee presented that autumn was notable in three respects.[225] It recommended for the Navy the introduction of an effective Two-Power Standard which would 'enable us to place a Fleet in the Far East fully adequate to act on the defensive and to serve as a strong deterrent to any threat to our interests,' as well as maintaining in Home Waters 'a force able to meet the requirements of war with Germany.' It reiterated the need for what was now, in deference to public susceptibilities, to be called not an Expeditionary Force but a Field Force, five divisions strong, to be available on the Continent within two weeks, with a follow-up force of 12 Territorial Divisions to reinforce it over a period of eight months. And it recommended that measures of industrial mobilization should be instituted to 'build up in peace-time reserves sufficient for a limited period after the outbreak of war and simultaneously plan and arrange our industrial capacity in peace-time so that in the interval assured by those reserves it is able to turn over to full war production.' Together with the new Air Ministry Scheme F for the construction by 1939 of a force of 1,736 first line aircraft, including nearly a thousand bombers with adequate reserves, these proposals constituted the first serious programme to enable the British Armed Forces to take part in a major war against their most probable adversaries.

These recommendations were in general approved by the Cabinet although they involved increases of expenditure over the next five years which could only be met by recourse to that most pernicious of expedients, a Defence Loan; and they were announced to the country in the Defence White Paper of 1936.[226] But one item still stuck in the throat of the Cabinet: the proposals for a Field Force with its train of Territorial Divisions to take part in a campaign on the Continent. The Cabinet challenged neither the political nor the military arguments of the Chiefs of Staff: they only said, almost unanimously, that the British public would not stand for it. Chamberlain led the attack; Baldwin allowed himself to be swept along unresisting; and even the new Foreign Secretary, Anthony Eden, spoke of the 'difficulty of getting the proposals for the Army approved by the House of Commons and the country.'[227] For the moment only the Regular Divisions of the Field Force were approved, without their Territorial Reinforcements, but even this decision was to stand for little more than twelve months.

For the most powerful member of Baldwin's Cabinet, the Chancellor of the Exchequer and Baldwin's heir apparent, Neville Chamberlain, remained implacably hostile to all idea of involvement on the Continent. When in December 1936 the War Office pointed out the illogicality of providing a Field Force but no reserves to back it up with, he sent a powerful memorandum from the Treasury.[228] This argued, first, that national resources were simply not adequate to provide for the Royal Navy, a powerful Air Force, the air defence of Great Britain, Imperial commitments, and an Army on a continental scale as well. It further pointed out that popular opinion, 'strongly opposed to continental adventures ... will be strongly suspicious of any preparation made in peace time with a view to large scale military operations on the Continent and they will regard such preparations as likely to result in our being entangled in disputes which do not concern us.' Opinions (it went on) 'will no doubt differ as to whether or not this almost instinctive aversion from large scale military preparations corresponds with a sound perception of the principles upon which our foreign policy should be founded. But at least it is a factor which can never be ignored by those responsible for framing our policies.' How much weight he thought it wise, rather than expedient, to allot to this factor, Chamberlain unfortunately did not say.

Chamberlain's financial and political calculations were so persuasive, and his enhanced influence after he became Prime Minister in May 1937 was so great, that by the end of the year the Cabinet had decided not only that the Territorial Army should not be equipped for continental intervention at all, but that the Field Force should not be either. There were, it is true, other important factors involved in this decision. The growth of German air power was to make necessary an ever greater diversion of resources to the air defence of Great Britain; including military man-power, both to man guns and searchlights, and to preserve order among what the Chiefs of Staff feared might be a panic-stricken civilian population. In the Mediterranean the Italian triumph over Abyssinia and over the League of Nations foreshadowed a new threat to Egypt; while the eruption of troubles in Palestine after 1936 not only pinned down eighteen battalions of the British Army in peace-keeping operations which showed no signs of ever coming to an end, but set off a wave of anti-British feeling throughout the Middle East of which the implications were incalculable. How could the British Army without expansion on a scale which would compete ruinously for resources with the other two Services, possibly handle these obligations and a continental commitment as well?[229]

When in December 1937 the new Minister for Co-ordination of Defence, Sir Thomas Inskip, presented to the Cabinet his list of priorities in defence obligations, he therefore allocated to the Army as its primary role 'the defence of Imperial commitments, including defence at home'; and only as a last objective 'which can only be provided after the other objectives have been met' did he list cooperation in 'the defence of the territories of any allies we may have in war'.*[230] In the Cabinet only Eden voiced 'some apprehensions as to our inability to help our allies on land' but even he agreed that 'the arguments of the Report appeared to him irresistible and the position was quite different from 1914.' For the Army Hore-Belisha declared 'he had no doubt it was right to put the continental commitment last . . . he thought that when the French realized that we could not commit ourselves to send an expedition they would be the more inclined to accelerate the extension of the Maginot Line to the sea.'[231] In February 1938 he reorganized the Field Force to provide simply two infantry and one mobile division 'equipped for an Eastern theatre'. These divisions, he stated, would be available for continental commitments 'only if the situation in the rest of the world permits, and it would be necessary for the General Staff to review the whole field

* He did warn that 'If France were again to be in danger of being overrun by land armies, a situation might arise when, as in the last war, we have to improvise our army to assist her. Should this happen, the Government of the day would most certainly be criticized for having neglected to provide against so obvious a contingency.'

of possible action open to the enemy before this could be determined.'[232] What was generally termed a policy of 'limited liability' in continental warfare had now shrunk to one of no liability at all.

What had happened to the Chiefs of Staff's arguments of 1934-5 about the vital need to hold Belgium as a protective glacis against air attack, and about the political importance of land forces fighting by the side of France? The reasons for the abandonment of the first of these points remains rather obscure. Certainly changes were occurring within the Air Ministry's programmes which made the Low Countries less essential to the defensive and offensive deployment of the Royal Air Force than they had been in 1934. In autumn 1937 the policy was initiated of equipping Bomber Command entirely with heavy bombers capable of reaching Germany from bases in the United Kingdom. Simultaneously the first RDF (Radar) stations were being erected along the east coast to give greatly advanced warning of the approach of enemy aircraft; and on the insistence of Inskip, in the teeth of Air Ministry resistance, fighter programmes were being accelerated.[233] The Royal Air Force was now developing weapons-systems which were beginning to make a foothold on the continent of Europe, from their point of view, expendable. Consciously or unconsciously this may have affected the attitude of the Air Staff to the continental commitment.

As to the political argument, the Chiefs of Staff had now totally reversed their position. The last thing they now wanted was any kind of involvement on the Continent which would, they feared, saddle them with obligations they could not possibly fulfil. When early in 1938 the Foreign Office suggested that exploratory staff conversations might be held with France and Belgium, the Chiefs of Staff replied with what a senior official of the Foreign Office termed with some reason 'an astounding document'. In this they suggested that 'the very term "staff conversations" has a sinister purport and gives an impression...of mutually assumed military collaboration.' The Army, they pointed out, had nothing to offer the French anyhow. Air conversations might be useful, they admitted, 'from a purely military point of view', but it would be unwise to hold them: the French would probably leak the news of them quite deliberately and so precipitate 'the very situation we wish to avoid, namely the irreconcilable suspicion and hostility of Germany.' Even naval talks about the Mediterranean they regarded as undesirable since 'If...France were in alliance with us against Italy, Germany would be almost certain to come in against us.' It is not surprising that after reading these recommendations Eden should have written to the Prime Minister: 'I cannot help believing that what the Chiefs of Staff would really like to do is to reorientate our whole foreign policy and to clamber on the bandwagon with the dictators, even though that process meant parting company with France and estranging our relations with the United States.'[234]

This verdict on the Chiefs of Staff though unkind, was not entirely unjust. 'What they would really like' they had, in fact, been stating with increasing urgency since the autumn of 1935. It was then that they had first suggested that it should be:

> a cardinal requirement of our national and imperial security that our foreign policy should be so conducted as to avoid the possible development of a situation in which we might be confronted simultaneously with the hostility, open or veiled, of Japan in the Far East, Germany in the West and any power on the main line of communication between the two.[235]

In December 1937 they had repeated this warning in even stronger terms.

> Without overlooking the assistance which we would hope to obtain from France and possibly other allies, we cannot foresee the time when our defence forces will be strong enough to safeguard our trade, territory and vital interests against Germany, Italy and Japan at the same time . . . they could not exaggerate the importance from the point of view of Imperial Defence of any political or international action which could be taken to reduce the number of our potential enemies and to gain the support of potential allies.[236]

Finally, in March 1938, when asked their views on the military implications of a possible German attack in Czechoslovakia, the Chiefs of Staff pointed out that Czechoslovakia's integrity could be restored only by defeating Germany in a prolonged struggle; that 'if such a struggle were to take place it is more than probable that both Italy and Japan would seize the opportunity to further their own ends, and that in consequence the problem we have to envisage is not that of limited European war only but of world war.' Such a world war they certainly did not, at present, have the resources to win.[237] Chamberlain was clearly not oblivious of this advice in his subsequent handling of the Czech situation.[238]

About these *démarches* of the Chiefs of Staff there are two things to be said. First, they were only asking the Government to do what its predecessors had done between 1902 and 1907: to extricate the country, by diplomatic manoeuvre, from the prospect of a conflict against a combination of adversaries which in their professional judgment could not be successfully sustained. But the world had changed since 1904. Britain's potential adversaries did not now include a France willing to purchase European security at the price of colonial expansion, or a Russian Empire torn by internal revolution and external defeat. They consisted of predatory powers who regarded appeasement as surrender and came back for more. Secondly, the twin obligations of Home Defence and Imperial Defence evidently now appeared so overriding that no forces could be spared to fulfil the third traditional aim of British Defence policy, an aim now regarded as totally archaic where it had not been completely forgotten: the maintenance of the European Balance of Power. But if that balance *were* to be overthrown, for how long would Home Defence be possible? and if Home Defence was not possible, what would then happen to the Empire?

6 The End of Empire, 1938-1942

When Chamberlain declared on his return from Munich in September 1938, that he had brought back 'Peace with Honour', there was little immediate inclination in the country as a whole to question the claim. The critics of the Munich settlement, especially those inside the Conservative Party, were for many months in an uncomfortable minority. The supporters of that settlement included, with the exception only of New Zealand, the Governments of all the Dominions. They included the broad masses who were simply and unaffectedly relieved that a war which had seemed imminent and unavoidable was not going to break out after all. They included all those guilt-ridden critics of the Versailles settlement, the Lothians, the Geoffrey Dawsons, who had for so long urged that only by doing justice to German claims for national self-determination could lasting peace be established in Europe. Munich was, as A. J. P. Taylor has so properly if so cruelly reminded us, 'a triumph for all that was best and most enlightened in British life.'[239] Those who denounced the settlement most strongly—Winston Churchill, Duff Cooper—did so on the grounds not so much of its immorality as of its disastrous implications for the power structure of Europe and for British security as a result. These old-fashioned and discredited arguments awoke little echo among the ranks of the Opposition. But more important and more interesting, they awoke even less among those professional guardians of British security, the Chiefs of Staff.

For the Chiefs of Staff headed the third group which supported the Munich settlement: those who believed that Britain was simply too weak to fight. The attitude of the military was summed up by General Ironside in his diary: 'Chamberlain is of course right. We have not the means of defending ourselves and he knows it. . . . We cannot expose ourselves now to a German attack. We simply commit suicide if we do.'[240] In their professional advice to the Cabinet in September the Chiefs of Staff repeated the warnings they had given the previous March. In the event of war, they stated, 'the restoration of Czechoslovakia's lost integrity could only be achieved by the defeat of Germany and as the outcome of a prolonged struggle, which from the outset must assume the character of an unlimited war.' This war was, they considered, likely to develop into a world war; and 'War against Japan, Germany and Italy simultaneously in 1938 is a commitment which neither the present nor the projected strength of our defence forces is designed to meet, even if we were in alliance with France and Russia, and which would therefore place a dangerous strain on the resources of the Empire.'[241]

Of more immediate significance, the Chiefs of Staff reported that the German Air Force was capable of maintaining a scale of attack on the United Kingdom of between 500 and 600 tons a day for the first two months of the war. To meet this attack, we now know, Fighter Command had 29 squadrons of which only five were equipped with modern aircraft (Hurricanes: no Spitfires were yet available). It had no adequate systems for fighter-control, communications or early warning. Of the ground defences of Anti-Aircraft Command—the guns, searchlights, the balloon barrage to prevent low-flying attacks on cities—about one third were ready at the most generous estimate.[242] As for British capacity to retaliate against Germany, the Chiefs of Staff rated it at 100 tons of bombs a day; but we have already seen how the Commander in Chief of Bomber Command considered, that autumn, that any operations involving deep penetration into Germany 'might end in major disaster.'[243]

It was this weakness in air defence that the Cabinet's military advisers, in September 1938, appear to have considered decisive. General Ismay, Hankey's successor as Secretary of the Committee for Imperial Defence, drew up on 22nd September—the day of Chamberlain's meeting with Hitler at Bad Godesberg, a week before the Munich meeting—a balance sheet of the comparative advantages of fighting Germany immediately or postponing the issue for a year.[244] If war were postponed, he agreed, Germany would increase her prestige, her war potential, her capacity to hold out against blockade, and the size and efficiency of her land forces: but 'even so, bearing in mind the advantage which the defensive has over the offensive in land warfare, and in particular the strength of the Maginot Line, she could hardly hope for a rapid decision on land.' But the improvement which the British could make in their air defences in the course of a year would more than make up for any increase in German air strength over the same period. 'By improving the United Kingdom's air defences,' he argued, 'and so substantially reducing Germany's chance of a rapid decision, we shall have provided a strong deterrent against her making the attempt.'

Given the narrow margin by which the Battle of Britain was in fact won two years later, when the effective strength of Fighter Command was nearly ten times as great and its radar installations were virtually complete, Ismay's calculations were probably right. Yet they did leave two factors out of account: the internal situation in Germany, and the unlikelihood that the Germans would initiate a war undertaken for the conquest of Czechoslovakia with an aerial knock-out blow against Britain.

On the first point it would be inappropriate to say much here. It is true that in the summer of 1918, when German power not only in Europe but in Asia appeared at its most terrifying, the régime was in fact on the verge of total collapse; a situation of which Allied intelligence, even in those days of comparatively open information, seems to have been completely unaware. It is also true that in 1938 a group of senior officers in the German Army were prepared to launch a *coup d'état* to remove Hitler from power rather than allow their country to be drawn into a world war for which it was, in their view, completely unprepared. But to argue from these facts that, but for the Munich settlement, Hitler might have been overthrown in 1938 is to take a considerable imaginative leap. The Wehrmacht was not, like the Reichswehr of the 1920s, a homogeneous body standing obediently behind its traditional leaders. A large number of its younger officers were now enthusiastic National Socialists whose loyalty to their Führer was a matter of conviction as well as oath. The party cadres were staunch; and among the German nation as a whole Hitler stood perhaps at the peak of his popularity. Under such conditions, what hope would a *putsch* launched by a small group of reactionary brass-hats have had of permanent success? The best that could be hoped was that in the confusion Hitler himself might have been killed, which would certainly have transformed the situation for the better. But the devil has a regrettably good record for looking after his own, and it was a slender expectation on which to build great decisions of war and peace.

The other criticism is more substantial. The British Chiefs of Staff had never been able to reconcile their conflicting views as to whether a war with Germany would start with a knock-out blow against England, as the Air Staff maintained, or whether, as the General Staff believed, Germany was still basically a land animal with its air forces geared to its army's requirements and its strategy directed towards achieving its national ambitions on the mainland of Europe, particularly in the East. As we now know, the Air Staff was wrong and the General Staff was right. The Luftwaffe had no doctrine of strategic bombing and no plans for a knock-out blow. The opportunity presented to it in August 1940 took the German Air Force completely by surprise, and its attacks on Britain were improvised and ill-coordinated. But in 1938 British intelligence reports of German intentions were conflicting, and it is neither surprising nor culpable that the Chiefs of Staff should have based their advice on the worst possible case. Had the Americans done the same before Pearl Harbour, under rather comparable conditions, the history of the War in the Far East might have been very different.

What is more surprising is the apparent failure of the Chiefs of Staff to take into account the implications which the surrender of 35 well-equipped Czech divisions would have for their doctrine of 'limited liability' in Europe. If that doctrine had been the product of strategic rather than simply financial calculation, it must have been based on the assumption that the French Army and its allies in Eastern Europe were capable on their own of holding the German land forces in check; an assumption which, it would seem, the French General Staff itself had hitherto made. But with the disappearance of those eastern allies—with the disappearance indeed of any effective Eastern Front—the strategic situation was transformed.

It would seem to have taken the British Government about three months to realize this. It was at a meeting of the Committee of Imperial Defence on 15th December that the Foreign Secretary, Lord Halifax, first tentatively suggested that 'a time might come when the French would cease to be enthusiastic about their relations with Great Britain if they were left with the impression that it was they who must bear the brunt of the fighting and slaughter on land.'[245] A week later the British Military Attaché in Paris indicated in a despatch that the time had come already.[246] France, without a dependable ally in Europe, now found herself faced by a Greater Germany with a population almost double her own which 'may see in the occasion an opportunity to deal with France and by so doing finally to prevent any interference with her own plans for expansion eastwards.' The French General Staff, he wrote, now looked to Britain to redress the balance, by providing the divisions lost to them in Central Europe; while French public opinion was unanimous in demanding from Britain, not simply the distant support of naval and air power, but—a sombre phrase—'*un effort du sang*'.

Within the next few weeks a flood of information poured into the Foreign Office confirming this advice. The French Ambassador himself invited the British to understand 'the feelings of a people who felt that they were going to have to stand all the casualties on land, where they would be a hundred times heavier than in the air and on the sea, and who knew very well in their heart that their manpower was not sufficient to hold their own with Italy and Germany at the same time.'[247] It was just such an appeal that had compelled Lord Kitchener in 1915 finally to commit the British Army to the Western Front with the comment 'one makes war, not as one would like to, but as one must.'

Once they appreciated the situation, the Chiefs of Staff carried out a remarkable volte-face. It was barely a year since they had accepted only as the last of their priorities 'co-operation in the defence of the territories of any allies we may have in war,' and since the War Office had insisted that a Field Force should go to the Continent 'only if the situation in the rest of the world permits, and it would be necessary for the General Staff to review the whole field of possible action open to the enemy before this can be determined.'[248] Now they acknowledged that 'France might give up the unequal struggle unless supported with the assurance that we should assist them to the utmost. If France were forced to her knees, the further prosecution of the war would be compromised. . . . It is difficult,' they admitted, rather belatedly, 'to say how the security of the United Kingdom could be maintained if France were forced to capitulate, and therefore defence of the former may have to include a share in the land defence of French territory.'[249] After fifteen years they had at last come back to the position first stated by Sir George Milne at the time of Locarno: Britain's frontier was on the Rhine.

In the Cabinet the defenders of limited liability did not put up much of a fight. Chamberlain himself first suggested that 'when the French know the whole position they would appreciate not only what a gigantic effort we had made but also that in the common interest our best course might be that we should not attempt to expand our land forces.'[250] But by the end of February even he was convinced. To meet the Army's demands for a Field Force six divisions strong, an immediate reserve of four Territorial Army divisions and full training equipment for the rest of the Territorial Army, would cost an additional £81 million; but Chamberlain admitted with frank reluctance that he could see no alternative and even Sir John Simon, the Chancellor of the Exchequer, agreed that 'other aspects of this matter outweighed finance.'[251] This time nobody seems to have made any difficulties about staff conversations with the French, which were authorized by the Cabinet at the beginning of February; and on 29th March, two weeks after Hitler's occupation of Czechoslovakia, these began.[252]

In exactly the same way as in the years before the First World War, political and military logic had forced reluctant British Ministers to the conclusion which they had for so long tried to evade: that the British Isles could only be defended on the Continent of Europe, and that in consequence a firm commitment to continental allies was inescapable. But this time the Government did not far outrun public opinion. As the German invasion of Belgium in August 1914 had resolved the differences between those who considered international affairs in terms of law and morality and those who saw them in terms of *Realpolitik*, so did Hitler's annexation of the non-German territories of Czechoslovakia on 15th March 1939. For the British people as a whole this day may be said to have marked the effective beginning of the Second World War: when, where and how hostilities would begin was a matter of tactical detail.

Recruits now began to pour into the Territorial Army, not to fight for the balance of power, not fired by the idealistic exhilaration of 1914, but in the belief that national survival was now threatened by an aggressive power inspired by a philosophy of nihilistic violence that had to be destroyed if it was not sooner or later to destroy them. The same consciousness was apparent in the Dominions. There public opinion, having lagged behind governments, now began to run ahead of them. Six months later when Britain declared war on Germany only in South Africa was public opinion seriously divided. In Australia and New Zealand hardly a voice was raised in protest when the Prime Ministers declared that British belligerence automatically involved their own countries. In Canada, Mr Mackenzie King declared the war to be 'a crusade', and the Canadian Parliament took their country into it without a division. And in all three Dominions it was again public pressure rather than Government initiative that led, in spite of all inter-war resolutions to the contrary, to the establishment of expeditionary forces to serve once again overseas under British command.[253]

In Britain the decision taken at the end of March to double the size of the Territorial Army from 13 to 26 Divisions was reached almost casually, by the Secretary of State for War and the Prime Minister, without even consulting the Chiefs of Staff. It was based partly on the need for additional man-power to place the anti-aircraft defences in a state of 24-hour readiness;[254] partly on the desire, as Simon expressed it in the Cabinet, to provide 'some impressive evidence of the prompt determination of our people, expressed in some very definite form.'[255] But it was also a response to public mood, and as such welcomed by virtually everyone outside the War Office, who had not been consulted about it and who had to improvise as wildly as they did for Kitchener's New Armies in 1914.

The introduction of compulsory military training during the course of the summer encountered, predictably enough, more difficulties, but there was nothing in the way of great popular opposition. Once again, this was a measure initiated by civilian ministers largely in response to public pressure. When the matter was first raised in the Cabinet on 22nd March, Lord Chatfield, who in January had succeeded Sir Thomas Inskip as Minister for Coordination of Defence, said, in a slightly bewildered fashion, 'that he did not think that the Defence Ministers or the Chiefs of Staff had ever considered what advantages could be derived from conscription.'[256] It is certainly doubtful whether the Army had faced the implications of, for the second time in a generation, transforming itself from a small professional force concerned primarily with Imperial Policing into a cadre to train and command a conscript force over a million strong to take part in large-scale continental warfare. It is even more doubtful whether it welcomed it. The task was enormous. The Field Force, which at the beginning of 1939 still consisted of 5 Regular divisions only, was by a stroke of the pen converted to 32 divisions, to which, when War broke out, a further 14 were added from the Dominions and 4 from India. During the course of the war the target rose yet higher, to 23 armoured and 73 infantry divisions.[257] With this expansion the War Office coped, on the whole, with intelligence, efficiency, and a remarkable degree of success; but it is not surprising that for many years British units were under-equipped and under-trained, commanded by officers promoted beyond their capacity and served by inexperienced staffs. In this respect at least Dunkirk was a mercy: it enable the bulk of the British Army to expand and train at leisure. But for that, the misfortunes which attended British arms in the early years of the war in Norway, Greece, Cyrenaica, Malaya and Singapore might have been repeated nearer home, on a larger scale, and with even more catastrophic results.

The acceptance of a continental commitment involved not only the creation of armed forces large enough to sustain it. It required also the formulation of a continental strategy; and that called for the reconstitution of an Eastern Front. On

18th March, three days after the German entry into Prague, the Cabinet agreed to approach the Soviet Union, Poland, Yugoslavia, Turkey, Greece and Rumania, to obtain assurances that these countries would join in resisting any act of aggression in Eastern Europe. The political object was frankly stated in Cabinet by Chamberlain two days later: 'The precise form which the *casus belli* might take is not perhaps very material. . . . We should attack Germany, not in order to save a particular victim, but in order to pull down the bully.'[258] But the General Staff had a more precise object in mind: to bar Germany's further advance towards South-East Europe. There she would not only obtain essential raw materials—the oil of Rumania, the ores of Yugoslavia—but be able to threaten the British position in the Eastern Mediterranean, to foment the smouldering discontent in the Arab countries, and perhaps ultimately to recreate the threat to the Indian Ocean that she had posed in the dark days of 1917–18. They therefore devoted rather less energy to plans for helping an inaccessible Poland than they did to negotiating for alliances with Turkey, Greece and Yugoslavia; countries which provided a glacis covering the Eastern Mediterranean, which could be sustained by British air and naval power based on the Middle East, and which might ultimately provide a valuable springboard for counterattacks—particularly from the air.[259] This policy was to be consistently pursued until 1941. It lay behind the ill-fated decision to go to the rescue of Greece, and it was not abandoned even after Greece and Yugoslavia had been overrun. Much effort continued to be expended in sustaining Resistance movements in Greece and Yugoslavia, and it was not until late in 1943 that attempts were abandoned to bring Turkey into the war.

As for the Soviet Union, the accusation that Chamberlain

did too little to woo her is probably fair. Certainly individual members of the Cabinet made no effort to conceal their reluctance to do so. When General Ironside told Neville Chamberlain on 10th July that to come to an understanding with Russia was the only thing they could do, Chamberlain replied 'The only thing we cannot do.'[260] Yet Chamberlain might well have been referring not so much to the undesirability as to the sheer difficulty of negotiating with that sullen and suspicious power. Those who pressed most eagerly for an alliance would have been the first to object to the political price which the Soviet Union was likely to exact in Eastern Europe; and no one could solve the fundamental difficulty of making military arrangements for the Soviet Army to assist in the defence of Poland when the Polish Government, for reasons which seemed adequate at the time and have lost none of their force since, was reluctant to allow Soviet forces to set foot on one inch of their soil. It is difficult logically to denounce both Britain's failure to reach agreement with the Soviet Union in 1939 and Britain's acquiescence in Soviet domination of Eastern Europe in 1945. In any case, Soviet military efficiency in the aftermath of the great purges was a totally unknown quantity. The British Intelligence appreciation at the time was that the Red Army might be effective in defending Russia itself but was unlikely to make much of a contribution beyond her borders; an assessment which the Russian military performance between December 1939 and December 1941 showed to err only on the side of generosity.

Thus a contribution by the Soviet Union barely figured in the plans for a war against Germany and Italy which the Chiefs of Staff completed in February 1939 as a basis for the forthcoming staff conversations with the French. This was an impressive document:[261] 90 pages long, containing 430 paragraphs covering every aspect of allied strategy and giving a remarkably accurate forecast of the way in which Germany was ultimately to be defeated; although it failed, understandably enough, to identify the Powers she was to be defeated by. This emphasized the need to get help to France as early as possible, irrespective of the size of the force despatched. It stressed the importance of holding Egypt as a base from which attacks could be launched against the weakest point in the enemy's defences, the Italian Empire. It recognized that the war would begin with a major enemy offensive and that all initial efforts would have to be directed to holding it. 'Our subsequent policy,' it concluded, 'should be directed to weakening Germany and Italy by the exercise of economic pressure and by intensive propaganda, while at the same time building up our major strength until we can adopt an offensive major strategy. Command of the sea would then confer freedom of choice in striking at the enemy's most vulnerable points. Once we had been able to develop the full fighting strength of the Empire, we should regard the outcome of the war with confidence.'

So much for Europe: but if Japan came into the war, the Chiefs of Staff admitted that they would be very much less confident. The despatch of a British fleet to Singapore would, they agreed, be imperative, and the French would have to be left to look after the Italian fleet in the Mediterranean. But 'The British Empire would be threatened simultaneously in Europe, the Mediterranean and the Far East by an immense aggregate of armed force, which neither our present nor our projected strength is designed to meet, with France as our only major ally. The outcome of the war would be likely to depend on our ability to hold on to our key positions and upon other Powers, particularly the United States, coming to our aid.'

Now this was almost the first mention, in any Chiefs of Staff document, of the possibility of American help, and it arose in the context of a war in the Pacific where such help was by no means unlikely. There was as yet no suggestion that the United States might become involved in a war in Europe, and no wonder. As soon as the situation in Europe had begun to look dangerous the Americans had put up the shutters with the Neutrality Act of 1935, which authorized the President to prohibit the sale of arms to belligerent nations, and bolted them with the Act of 1937 which compelled him to do so. There was no reason to suppose that the United States would extend any facilities whatever to the Allies except permission to purchase such raw materials as they could pay for, cash on the barrel, and carry home.

And how much could be paid for? This was a problem which haunted the Treasury, and with very good reason. In the whole story of British rearmament the Treasury had played a vital, indeed the dominant role. Since no pre-war Prime Minister was likely to overrule its advice—certainly not when so formidable a figure as Neville Chamberlain inhabited No. 11 Downing Street—it was with the Treasury that responsibility really lay for reconciling the apparently contradictory responsibilities: nursing Britain's convalescent economy back to health, and equipping her with the military resources she needed to play her part as a major actor in the international system. As we now know, the task appeared to be even more difficult than it was owing to their deep-seated reluctance to have recourse to anything in the nature of deficit financing. In fact, as Dr Schacht was demonstrating in Germany to the dismay of liberal and socialist economists alike, large rearmament programmes could have a most stimulating effect on stagnant industrial economies. But the most expert financial wizardry could have done no

more than mitigate the fundamental problem as Sir Warren
Fisher defined it for the Defence Requirements Committee
in 1934: 'Raw materials [not to mention food] are only
produced within this country in relatively negligible quanti-
ties and therefore have to be secured from other countries
who will not of course give us them, and when our international purchasing power is exhausted, will not continue
indefinite credits to us.'[262]

Britain's resources were limited, and in her rearmament
programme she faced a genuine problem of resource alloca-
tion which compelled a choice between a force-structure
capable of sustaining the burden of Imperial Defence and
one which would carry effective political weight on the
Continent. Chamberlain's aversion to a continental commitment grew out of his six-year struggle, as Chancellor of
the Exchequer, to tailor the defence programme to what the
Treasury believed the capacity of the national economy to be.
'In my view,' he wrote in his diary on 25th October 1936,
'we had not the manpower to produce the necessary munitions for ourselves and perhaps, if the United States stood
out, for our Allies, to man the enlarged Navy, the new Air
Force, and a million-man Army.'[263] It is by no means clear
that he was wrong. If a long war was visualized he was
almost certainly *not* wrong. For in such a war, as Inskip
pointed out the following year, 'If we are to emerge vic-
toriously . . . it is essential that we should enter it with
sufficient economic strength to enable us to make the fullest
use of resources overseas and to withstand the strain.' Maintenance of economic stability, he considered, was therefore
an element in defensive strength 'which can properly be
regarded as a fourth arm in defence . . . without which
purely military effort would be of no avail.'[264]

The somewhat belated realization at the beginning of

1939, that it was of little use to husband resources to sustain a long war if the enemy was able to defeat you in a short one, did not invalidate this reasoning. The Treasury did open its purse strings in the last half of the decade. The annual expenditure on rearmament rose from £60 m. in 1936 to £182.2 m. in 1938, and to £273 m. in 1939. Income tax during this period rose from 5s. 6d. to 7s. 6d. in the pound. A five year Defence Loan of £400 millions was launched in 1937, and doubled two years later.[265] But these measures even had they been twice as draconic, could not solve the balance of payments problem. Early in 1940 the Treasury reported that the United Kingdom was running an adverse balance of payments which by the end of the year was likely to total £400 m., whereas her total disposable resources— gold reserves and marketable securities—came to no more than £700 m. Those resources which, if prudently husbanded, might just last for three years, would at the existing rate of expenditure be exhausted before the end of two.[266]

Almost the first message which Mr Churchill sent to President Roosevelt when he assumed office as Prime Minister in May 1940 consisted of an explanation of this problem, with the assurance 'We shall go on paying dollars for as long as we can, but I should like to feel reasonably sure that when we can pay no more you will give us the stuff just the same.'[267] President Roosevelt did indeed give him the stuff, thanks to Lend-Lease legislation; but in 1939 there was no reason to expect that transformation in American public opinion over the next two years which would make it possible for him to do so. The only sensible view to take at that stage was that expressed by the Treasury representative at a meeting to consider the strategic appreciation of the Chiefs of Staff in April 1939: 'If we were under the impression that we were as well able as in 1914 to conduct a long war, we were burying our heads in the sand.'[268] But if Britain could *not* conduct a long war, what kind of a war could she conduct?

No pre-war plans for a European war, then, could take the United States into account, either as a direct or as an indirect ally. But France was taken very much into account; and with France as an ally the tensions between European and Imperial commitments became less acute in one respect at least. France could help take the strain in the Mediterranean.

Ever since the Abyssinian crisis the Royal Navy knew very well that it could not at the same time contain the Italian fleet in the Mediterranean and provide the capital fleet promised to Singapore in the event of hostilities breaking out with Japan. During that crisis, as we have already seen, they had been inclined to give to the Far East an overriding priority; and this was the burden of the Chiefs of Staffs' statements at the Imperial Conference in 1937. The actual strength of the Fleet they could send, they then warned, would be governed by the situation obtaining in home waters; but they laid it down that 'the security of the United Kingdom and the security of Singapore would be the keystones on which the survival of the British Commonwealth was based.'[269] And they simultaneously urged on the Government recognition of the principle 'that no anxieties or risks connected with our interests in the Mediterranean can be allowed to interfere with the despatch of a fleet to the Far East.'[270]

But by the following year the situation had altered. In autumn 1938 the British found themselves confronted simultaneously with a major insurrection in Palestine, with all that implied for their position in the Arab world, and with a threat of war in Europe. In October the Chiefs of Staff had to advise that 'the first commitment of our land forces, after the security of the United Kingdom, shoud be the security of Egypt and of our interests in the Middle East.'[271] At the same time the Foreign Secretary was warning British diplomats in the Far East that Britain could bring no influence to bear to check the Japanese onslaught on South China or the establishment of her New Order in Asia. 'The plain fact is,' wrote Halifax, 'that Ministers feel unwilling at this moment to take any chance of provoking an incident with Japan which would face us with the choice of climbing down or depleting our forces in European waters, for we are not in a position effectively to defend our interests in the Far East at the moment. . . .'[272] The situation in Europe, in short, made it as impossible for Britain to intervene effectively in the Far East as her weakness in the Far East made it, in the view of the Chiefs of Staff, impossible for her to risk involvement in Europe. Such was the price of World Power!

The events of 1939 brought Britain no relief in her dilemma. Indeed, her diplomatic initiatives with Turkey and the Balkan Powers now made the maintenance of effective and reassuring naval strength in the Mediterranean even more important than it had been in the past. In April the Naval Staff reexamined the situation and came up with the following comment:

> it is not open to question that [in the event of Japanese intervention] a capital ship force would have to be sent [to the Far East] but whether this could be done to the exclusion of our interests in the Mediterranean is a matter which would have to be decided at the time. . . . The effect of the evacuation of the Eastern Mediterranean on Greece, Turkey and the Arab and Moslem world [they went on, unconsciously echoing Kitchener's fears of 1915] are political factors which make it essential that no precipitate action should be taken in this direction. . . . It is not possible to state definitively how soon after Japanese

intervention a Fleet can be despatched to the Far East. Neither is it possible to enumerate precisely the size of Fleet that we could afford to send.'[273]

In the light of this grim appreciation, the Chiefs of Staff could only advise that war in the Far East should be avoided for as long as possible: that 'without the active cooperation of the United States of America it would not be justifiable, from the military point of view, having regard to the existing international situation, to take any avoidable action which might lead to hostilities with Japan.'[274]

During the first year of the war the problem did not become urgent. Italy remained neutral, France assisted in the policing of the Mediterranean, and Japan was quiescent. But in the summer of 1940 it became inescapable. Italy entered the war; France collapsed, leaving Britain alone in the Mediterranean; and Japan began to move purposefully south, to gather the fruit from the branches of the imperial trees whose trunks had been so conveniently sawn through by the German victory in Western Europe. Within a few weeks the entire British strategy for the defence of her Empire in the Far East, so painstakingly erected in the face of so many obstacles over the past twenty years, lay in ruins. That strategy had rested on the assumption that the threat to Singapore would be naval and that it could be countered by the despatch of an adequate fleet. With the Japanese move southward into Tonkin in September 1940 and the fear —to be fulfilled the following year—of a further move into Cochin China, the threat became one of amphibious attack under land-based air cover. The arrival of a British capital fleet even if there was one available to send—and there was not, nor could there be until 1942 at the earliest—would no longer be decisive. Now Singapore could be defended only if the Malay peninsula was defended, and for this what was needed was troops and, even more urgently than troops, air cover and ground defence.[275]

Of these the deficiencies were enormous. In October 1940, of the 582 aircraft he needed to defend Malaya, Burma and Singapore, the General Officer Commanding Far East had 48.[276] The only reinforcements available were machines of obsolescent types, and even with these he was, a year later, still short of his target by 156—and comparably short in all other types of equipment. Adequate reinforcements might have been found by stripping the Middle East, and in Spring 1941 the Chiefs of Staff urged that this should be done. They reminded the Prime Minister of the frequent assurances which the British Government had given the Australians, that if Australian security were threatened the British would abandon all their interests in the Mediterranean and go to their aid. They emphasized that no such aid could be given if Singapore was lost. And the Chief of Imperial General Staff, Sir John Dill, declared his own belief 'that if we reach a point where the maintenance of our position in Egypt would endanger either the United Kingdom or Singapore we should hold fast to the latter, even if it meant the loss of Egypt.'[277]

The Prime Minister was adamant; and this was one of the very few issues during the entire course of the war on which he overruled his military advisers. The likelihood of Japan entering the war, he insisted, was still remote; if she did, the United States would almost certainly come in as well, and meanwhile, there was no need to go beyond the 'modest arrangements' already in hand for the defence of Malaya and Singapore. The loss of Egypt and the Middle East, on the other hand, he considered would be a disaster to Great Britain second only to successful invasion and final conquest.

'It is not to be expected,' he wrote, 'that the British forces of the land, sea and air would wish to survive so vast and shameful a defeat as would be entailed by our expulsion from Egypt.'[278]

Churchill's decision was perhaps not dictated by strategic factors alone. He knew little of the Far East; he had been hostile to the building of the Singapore base; and he may well have felt that in this part of the world British power could never be effective without American support. But he had served with Kitchener in Egypt; he had been one of the architects—indeed he had some claim to be the principal architect—of Britain's Empire in the Middle East after the First World War. This for him was, after India, the very heartland of the British Empire, worth retaining for its own sake irrespective of its significance in the conduct of the war. The generals who failed to defend it earned his malevolence; those who succeeded, his extravagant affection.

Yet even if Churchill had decided otherwise, and British strength in the summer of 1941 had been devoted to reinforcing the Far East rather than to preparing a counterattack in the Western Desert, it is unlikely that the outcome at Singapore would have been very different. The Japanese owed their victories, not to superiority in numbers of men or equipment but, like the Germans in 1940, to a command of military skills and virtues which the British and British-led forces opposing them simply did not, at that stage of the war, possess to a comparable degree. Singapore surrendered on 15th February 1942, and some 130,000 prisoners passed into Japanese hands. The charisma on which British rule in the East had rested for a hundred years and which British defence planners had been so anxious to preserve was destroyed for ever.

In February 1912, exactly thirty years before the fall of

Singapore, Winston Churchill had written: 'If the power of
Great Britain were shattered upon the sea, the only course
open to the five million white men in the Pacific would be to
seek the protection of the United States.'[279] Mr Curtin of
Australia for one did not hesitate for long. In the last days of
1941 he had already written in a newspaper article: 'Australia
looks to America, free from any pangs as to traditional links
or kinship with the United Kingdom.'[280] When in January
1942 Churchill set up a 'Pacific Council' in London to conduct the war in the Far East, even New Zealand rebelled, its
Prime Minister instead demanding 'direct and continuous
access to the power which . . . is solely responsible for the
conduct of naval operations in that part of the world which
includes New Zealand.'[281] Two months later his desire was
granted. Operational responsibility for the entire Pacific
area was taken over by the American Joint Chiefs of Staff,
and from that day to this Australia and New Zealand have
looked not to London but to Washington to assure their
defence. British forces were to go on fighting, with growing
skill and success, in the Far East, but they were fighting
neither to defend nor to repossess the British Empire: the
campaign in Burma was undertaken primarily to reopen the
overland route to China, which American strategists considered necessary to the activation of China as a base from
which United States forces could mount an attack on Japan.
They were based on an India about whose complete independence as soon as the war was over nobody, after the Cripps
Mission in March 1942, had any doubt. And if India did *not*
achieve independence, it would not be for any lack of pressure and encouragement from the United States.

Australia and New Zealand were not the first parts of the
British Empire to transfer from the British to the American
defensive system. In August 1940, Mackenzie King had met

President Roosevelt at Ogdensburg and out of their discussions developed the arrangements for Hemisphere Defence which have also survived, with necessary modifications, until the present day.[282] And even before this occurred, the United States had taken the first steps towards underwriting the security of the United Kingdom itself.

It was some measure of the reluctance of the British public to become involved in continental warfare at all that the evacuation of the British Army from Dunkirk, routed and weaponless as it was, should have been welcomed almost as a major victory. 'Personally I feel happier now that we have no allies to be polite to and pamper,' wrote George VI to his mother, 'and in these sentiments,' suggests his biographer 'he was at one with the vast majority of his subjects.'[283] Agreeable as such sentiments may have been, they were totally illusory, and they were shared neither by the Prime Minister nor by the Chiefs of Staff. If Britain was to survive for long, it was necessary for her to be very polite indeed to the United States, even if she was in no position to pamper her. In May 1940 the Chiefs of Staff produced a gallant strategic appreciation which still looked forward to the defeat of Germany 'by a combination of economic pressure, air attacks on economic objectives in Germany and on German morale, and the creation of widespread revolt in her conquered territories.' But all this rested on the assumption 'that we could count on the full economic and financial support of the United States, possibly extending to active participation on our side.' This appreciation was summarized for the use of the United States Government, and the British Ambassador in Washington was authorized to inform the President that 'without the full economic and financial cooperation of the whole of the American Continent, the task might in the event prove too great for the British

Empire single-handed. Nevertheless, even if the hope of victory in these circumstances appeared remote we should continue to fight as long as it was humanly possible to do so.'[284]

Once Winston Churchill had become Prime Minister there was no cause for anyone to doubt this last assurance. Nevertheless the capacity of Britain to stay in the war now depended—long before the United States joined her as a belligerent—on decisions taken in Washington: decisions to make available first arms, then credits to purchase them with, then shipping to transport them, then naval protection for the shipping; until by the autumn of 1941 American resources were firmly pledged to British victory. It might be argued that Churchill's greatest achievement lay not so much in the leadership he provided for his own countrymen as in the clarity with which he saw, from the very beginning of his Administration, that Britain was now dependent on the United States for her continued survival, and in the patience, the skill, the tenacity and the charm with which he coaxed the American people and their President into underwriting British independence. In so doing the United States assumed the burden of world responsibility which had at last grown too heavy for the United Kingdom to bear. Churchill had not, he asserted, become the King's First Minister in order to preside over the liquidation of the British Empire. Yet this was precisely what he had to do; and he did it with such panache that many years were to pass before it became generally apparent that the British Empire had come to an end, almost as imperceptibly as it had begun.

There were of course those who saw in the American Alliance, not the end of the British Empire, but its apotheosis; that final uniting of the Anglo-Saxon world to which

Rhodes and Milner had looked forward, which would at last enable Britain to rise above the confusion and commitments of European politics and which would provide a solid superstructure for world peace. To believe this was sadly to misjudge the temper of the United States. America was prepared to go to great lengths, if not indeed in the last resort to fight, to maintain the independence of the United Kingdom and the White Dominions; but she had no interest whatever in maintaining the British Empire, particularly in India or in the Middle East.

Nor did American strategists share Britain's aversion to a continental strategy. They were indeed quite emphatic that the war could not be won without one. To the strategic discussions which occupied the Combined Chiefs of Staff from 1942 until 1944 the Americans added to the British formula of bombing, subversion and blockade an insistence on a massive physical invasion of Europe which required once again the raising, training and deployment of ground forces on a scale, and for a battlefield, which British statesmen and soldiers had tried for two decades to avoid. It is not surprising that the American Joint Chiefs read into all the objections which their British colleagues raised to such a programme either a preference for a strategy which would safeguard their Imperial possessions, or the memories of the First World War.

But they were being less than fair. In Churchill's preference for fighting in the Mediterranean—the last theatre in which an Imperial Army under British commanders was winning spectacular victories—one can trace, as I have suggested elsewhere,[285] a strong element of nostalgia as well as a tinge of *Realpolitik*. If the British were to appear as equal partners at the peace table, the capture of Vienna by General Alexander's armies would strengthen their hand against both their giant allies. But the objections of the Chiefs of Staff to an attack in North West Europe which they regarded as premature rested on genuine military considerations whose validity has now been generally recognized. It was rather shortage of landing-craft than memories of Passchendaele that delayed the landings in Normandy until the summer of 1944.

After the Second World War neither the political nor the military leaders of the United Kingdom shrank any longer from a continental commitment. They had learned their lesson; though it was not until 1954, ten years after the Normandy landings, that a final, binding commitment was undertaken to maintain substantial British armed forces on the Continent in time of peace. We are unlikely ever again to have statesmen—or, come to that, strategists—who maintain that the security of the United Kingdom can be considered in isolation from that of our Continental neighbours east as well as west of the Rhine. It is now only rarely that we catch a faint, Curzonion echo from the occasional Prime Minister who maintains that our true frontier still rests on the Himalayas.

Notes to Chapters

Chapter 1

1. G. P. Gooch and Harold Temperley (ed.): *British Documents on the Origins of the War 1898–1914*, vol. III, p 430. Memorandum of 25th February 1907.

2. Sir Keith Hancock: *Smuts*, vol. I: *The Sanguine Years 1870–1919* (Cambridge 1962) p 108.

3. Julian Amery: *The Life of Joseph Chamberlain*, vol. IV (London 1951) p 421.

4. L. S. Amery: *My Political Life*, vol. I (London 1953) p 99.

5. ibid., p 192.

6. Arthur J. Marder: *British Naval Policy 1880–1905* (London 1940) pp 469–72.

7. ibid., p 428.

8. David Dilks: *Curzon in India*, vol. I (London 1969) p 170.

9. George Monger: *The End of Isolation* (London 1963) p 64.

10. Dilks, op. cit., p 113.

11. Quoted in A. P. Thornton: *The Imperial Idea and its Enemies* (London 1959) p 145, from *The Nineteenth Century*, January 1908.

12. Dilks, op. cit., p 30.

13. Amery, op. cit., p 35.

14. 'The Place of India in the Empire'. Address to the Philosophical Institute of Edinburgh, October 1909.

15. Sir Charles Dilke and Spenser Wilkinson: *Imperial Defence* (London 1892) p 102.

16. 'The Place of India in the Empire', p 14.

17. 'Frontiers': the Romanes Lectures in the University of Oxford, 1909.

18. '*Qui procul hinc*', the legend's writ,—
    The frontier-grave is far away—
    '*Qui ante diem periit*:
    Sed miles, sed pro patria.'
    'Clifton Chapel' in Henry Newbolt,
Poems New and Old (London 1912).

19. Monger, op. cit., p 110.

20. Dilks, op. cit., p 113.

21. M. V. Brett (ed): *Journals and Letters of Reginald Viscount Esher* (London 1934) vol. II, p 80.

22. Thornton, op. cit., p 97.

23. Sir Charles Lucas, *The Empire at War* (London 1921-6) vol. I, p 57.

24. ibid., p 58.

25. Anon. *The British Army*: by a Lieutenant Colonel in the British Army (London 1899).

26. Dilks, op. cit., pp 166, 177.

27. 'Military Needs of the Empire in a War with France and Russia' by Lt. Col. E. A. Altham, 12th August 1901, CID I.A., CAB 3/1/1A.

28. Committee of Imperial Defence, 57th Meeting, CAB 2/2/1.

29. Dilks, op. cit., p 206. For Clarke's scathing comments on Kitchener's proposals see Lord Sydenham of Combe: *My Working Life* (London 1927) pp 197-201.

30. Report of the Sub-Committee on the Military Requirements of the Empire - India (Morley Committee) 1st May 1907. CID 98—D.

31. Committee of Imperial Defence, 85th Meeting, CAB 2/2/1.

32. For all this agitation see Howard Moon, 'The Invasion of the United Kingdom: Public Controversy and Official Planning' (Ph.D. thesis for the University of London, 1968) and Marder, op. cit., pp 375–80.

33. CAB 3/1/1A, and 3/1/18A. Moon, op. cit., pp 221–44. The conclusion was confirmed by the incoming Liberal Government. At the Committee of Imperial Defence Meeting on 9 March 1906 'The Committee considered that, in view of the conclusion that a serious invasion of the United Kingdom is impossible, so long as our naval supremacy is maintained, the London defences should be abolished.' CID 85th Meeting. CAB 2/2/1.

34. Monger, op. cit., p 95.

35. *Esher, Journals*, vol. II, p 75.

36. *Cambridge History of the British Empire*, vol. II (London 1940) p 839. Richard A. Preston, *Canada and 'Imperial Defence'* (Duke University Press 1967) p 88.

37. Quoted by Lt. Col. E. A. Altham in 'Military Needs of the Empire in a War with France and Russia' (n. 27 above).

38. Preston, op. cit., p 122.

39. Parliamentary Papers 1887, LVI: C-5091.–I. Vol. II pp 327, 338.

40. Donald C. Gordon, *The Dominion Partnership in Imperial Defence* (Baltimore 1965) p 92.

41. Preston, op. cit., pp 362–70. *Cambridge History of the British Empire*, vol. III (London 1959) p 586.

42. See *Cambridge History of the British Empire*, vol. III, ch. XI: 'The Development of the Imperial Conference 1887–1914', *passim*.

43. Gordon (op. cit., p 139) shows the degree to which the agitation in Canada was whipped up by British agents, but this does not seem to have characterized developments in Australia or New Zealand. Preston (op. cit., p 265) while describing the colonial contributions as 'qualified, limited, hesitant and declining' considers that they had domestic effects 'out of all proportion to the effort made or to the degree in which they were involved.'

44. Cd. 3523. (1907) pp v, 94–128. Cd. 3524 (1907) pp 18–27.

45. Cd. 4948 (1909) p 19.

46. Monger, op. cit., p 79.

Chapter 2

47. For voluminous evidence on this, see Fritz Fischer: *Griff nach der Weltmacht* (Düsseldorf 1962) and Jonathan Steinberg: *Yesterday's Deterrent: Tirpitz and the birth of the German Battle Fleet* (London 1965).

48. See particularly Andreas Hillgruber: *Hitlers Strategie: Politik und Kriegfuhrung 1940–41* (Frankfurt a/m. 1965).

49. Randolph S. Churchill: *Winston S. Churchill*, vol. II (London 1969). Companion, pt. 3, p 1607.

50. A. J. Marder: *From the Dreadnought to Scapa Flow* (London 1961) vol. I, p 107.

51. See above, p 20, and Lord Esher to Edward VII on 21st Jan. 1907: 'The peace requirements of India govern and cover the military needs of the Empire, inasmuch as a war with Russia on the North West Frontier being the gravest military operation which your Majesty's Army could be called upon to undertake, covers by its

magnitude all other conceivable operations.' *Esher Journals*, vol. II, p 217.

52. Zara Steiner: *The Foreign Office and Foreign Policy 1898–1914* (Cambridge 1969) pp 70–94.

53. Memorandum by Lt. Col. William Robertson of 20 March 1906, quoted by N. W. Summerton: 'British Military Preparations for a War Against Germany.' (Ph.D. thesis for the University of London, 1969) p 159.

54. Quoted in Max Beloff: *Imperial Sunset: Britain's Liberal Empire 1897–1921*, vol. I (London 1969) p 184.

55. C. E. Callwell: *Field Marshal Sir Henry Wilson, His Life and Diaries* (London 1927) vol. I, p 323.

56. Hansard, Commons Debates, 3rd Ser., vol CXCI, 26th March 1868, col. 326.

57. 'It will be distinctly understood that the probability of the employment of an Army Corps in the field in any European War is sufficiently improbable to make it the primary duty of the military authorities to organize our forces efficiently for the defence of this country.' This document is printed in the Report of the Royal Commission on the War in South Africa, Cd. 1789 (1903) p 31.

58. CAB/1/1A.

59. Quoted in Sir William Robertson: *Soldiers and Statesmen* (London 1926) vol. I, p 20.

60. See the memorandum by Colonel Callwell quoted on p 42.

61. Quoted in N. W. Summerton, op. cit., p 163.

62. General Staff Memorandum of 2nd June 1908, CAB/1/7/740.

63. Letter to Lloyd George, 22nd May 1908, *Esher Journals*, vol. II, p 314. That Esher himself knew, or was soon to know, of the alternative possibilities, is shown by his entry for 1st October 1908: 'The King has *in Great Britain*, a force of 200,000 men which could be ready in

3 weeks, and possibly 18 days, to fight on the line of the Marne.' ibid., vol. II, p 350.

64. Parliamentary Debates (Fourth Ser.) vol. CXLVI, 11th May 1905, cols. 62–84.

65. On this literature see Moon, op. cit., and I. F. Clarke: *Voices Prophesying War* (London 1966) pp 137–58.

66. Parliamentary Debates (Fourth Ser.) vol. CXCVI, 23rd November 1908, cols. 1679–1743.

67. Parliamentary Debates (Official Report) House of Lords, 13th July 1909, col. 460; House of Commons, 24th May 1909, col. 812.

68. Amery: *My Political Life*, vol. I, p 332.

69. Churchill, op. cit., vol. II, Companion pt. 3, p 1500.

70. Arnold-Forster Diary (Add. MSS. 50339) 5th August 1904: quoted in N. J. d'Ombrain: 'The Military Departments and the Committee of Imperial Defence 1902–1914.' (Bodleian Library Ms. D.Phil. d. 4746.)

71. D'Ombrain, op. cit., p. 157.

72. General Sir Ian Hamilton: *Compulsory Service* (London 1910).

73. Conclusions of Committee of Imperial Defence Meeting, 22nd October 1908, CID 102nd Meeting, CAB 2/2/3.

74. M. P. A. Hankey: *The Supreme Command* (London 1961) vol. I, p 137.

75. Summerton op. cit., p 85 and Samuel R. Williamson: *The Politics of Grand Strategy: Britain and France prepare for War, 1904–1914* (Cambridge, Mass. 1969) p 48.

76. WO 33/364.

77. WO 106/46/E2.10.

78. A. J. Marder: *British Naval Policy* 1880–1905, p 504.

79. Williamson, op. cit., pp 50–1.

80. Notes of a Conference held at Whitehall Gardens, 19th December 1905, CAB/18/24. D'Ombrain op. cit., pp 132–6.

81. Julian S. Corbett: *Some Principles of Maritime Strategy* (London 1911). For the background and membership of this committee see Hankey: *The Supreme Command*, vol. I, p 39. Its report is printed in P. K. Kemp (ed.): *The Papers of Admiral Sir John Fisher* (Navy Records Society, London 1960) vol. II.

82. On this see John Gooch: 'The Origin and Development of the Imperial and General Staffs to 1916' (Ph.D. thesis for the University of London, 1969) and Summerton, op. cit., pp 360–2.

83. The emphasis given to this meeting has been very largely due to the significance attached to it by two articulate participants, Churchill and Lloyd George. See W. S. Churchill: *The World Crisis 1911–1914* (London 1923) pp 56–64 and Lloyd George: *War Memoirs*, vol. I (London 1933) p 51.

84. The proceedings of this Sub-Committee are in CAB 16/5, and have been thoroughly examined in Williamson, op. cit., pp 108–12.

85. CAB 16/5, Appendix VII.

86. Marder: *From Dreadnought to Scapa Flow*, vol. I, p 392.

87. Fisher to McKenna, 20th August, 1911: 'REST ASSURED that if the Government land a single British soldier in France (*or even entertain any plans for it!*) there will be an upheaval in England that will cast them out of office.' Quoted in Williamson, op. cit., p 187.

88. 'Crewe and Harcourt and Morley, who might be expected to take the naval point of view, were excluded,' Hankey reported to Fisher. (Marder: *Dreadnought to Scapa Flow*, vol. I, p 392). Hankey further suggests that Henry Wilson's cross-examination 'was not so severe as it would have been had Morley been present.' (*Supreme Command*, vol. I, p 80.)

89. 1st and 15th November. Asquith - George V. 16th November 1911. (Bodleian Library, Asquith MSS.Ms.6.)

90. Marder, op. cit., vol. I, pp 41, 72.

91. D. Facey-Crowther: 'British Military Planning and the Defence of Egypt' (Ph.D. thesis for the University of London, 1969) p 369.

92. Churchill, op. cit., vol. II, Companion pt. 3, p 1593.

93. *Esher Journals*, vol. III, pp 95–100. See further, for Esher's views, Marder, op. cit., vol. I, pp 291–4.

94. Marder, op. cit., vol. I, pp 289–90.

95. C.I.D., 4th July 1912, 117th Meeting, CAB 2/2/3.

96. Preston, *Canada and 'Imperial Defence'*, p 388ff. Gordon: *The Dominion Partnership*, p 223ff.

97. C.I.D., 30th May 1911, 113th Meeting, CAB 2/2/3.

98. C.I.D., 11th May 1911, 111th Meeting, CAB 2/2/3.

Chapter 3

99. *Esher Journals*, vol III, p 175. Stephen Roskill: *Hankey: Man of Secrets*, vol. I (London 1970) p 103.

100. C. E. Callwell: *Field Marshal Sir Henry Wilson*, vol. I, p 158.

101. Gerhard Ritter: *The Schlieffen Plan* (London 1958) p 162.

102. Sir James Edmonds: *History of the Great War based on Official Documents: Military Operations, France and Belgium 1914* (London 1933) vol. I, p 499.

103. ibid, p 264.

104. Hankey: *The Supreme Command*, vol. I, p 267.

105. Robert Blake (ed.): *The Private Papers of Douglas Haig 1914–1919* (London 1952) p 102.

106. Callwell: *Wilson*, vol. I, p 206.

107. Sir Charles Lucas: *The Empire at War*, vol. V, p 165.

108. Hankey: *The Supreme Command*, vol. II, p 460.

109. See Callwell: *Wilson*, vol. I, p 234. When Wilson urged Kitchener to abandon the Dardanelles 'he said it would mean trouble in India, loss of Egypt, in addition to loss of whole force while attempting to do it.'

110. Lucas: *The Empire at War*, vol. II, pp 84–7; vol. III, pp 114–26; vol IV, p 232.

111. Richard A. Preston: *Canada and 'Imperial Defence'*, p 512.

112. A. M. Gollin: *Proconsul in Politics: A Study of Lord Milner in Opposition and in Power* (London 1964) p 396.

113. W. K. Hancock: *Smuts: The Sanguine Years*, p 431.

114. Preston: op. cit., p 521.

115. L. S. Amery: *My Political Life*, vol. II, p 102.

116. See for example the minutes of the Cabinet Committee on War Policy, 10th Meeting, 21st June 1917. (Milner's copy, with his marginal annotations, is in the Bodleian Library: Milner Papers, 125 AE I.)

117. Lucas: *Empire at War*, vol. II, p 193; vol. III, p 147. Even Sir Charles Lucas's rather uncritical account records that 'the name of Passchendaele still arouses bitter memories in Canada.' Hankey: *Supreme Command*, vol. II, pp 829, 834. Callwell: *Wilson*, vol. I, p 119. Preston, op. cit., pp 490, 521.

118. *History of the Great War Based on Official Documents: Military Operations: Egypt and Palestine*, vol. I (London 1928) p 250.

119. ibid., vol. II, p 259.

120. Amery, op. cit., p 161.

121. ibid., pp 115–17. Leonard Stein: *The Balfour Declaration* (London 1961) pp 520–1.

122. Callwell: *Wilson*, vol. II, p 148.

123. Minutes of the Eastern Committee of the War Cabinet, EC 40th Meeting, 2nd December 1918, Annex. (In Milner Papers, Bodleian Library, 119).

124. loc. cit. Minutes of 42nd Meeting, 9th December 1918, Annex.

125. Unsigned Memorandum, 'The Eastern Theatre' of 25th March 1918. (In Milner Papers, 124 AD. Memorandum, 'The German Cause in the East' by E. Branch, Versailles, E/14. SWC 209. 11th May 1918, loc. cit.)

126. Richard H. Ullman: *Anglo-Soviet Relations 1917–1921: Intervention and the War* (Princeton 1961) p 311. Lucas: *British Empire at War*, vol. V, p 118.

127. Memorandum by the Chief of the Imperial General Staff, 25th July 1918. *Military Operations in France and Belgium*, vol. IV, pp 527–48.

128. For these operations see Ullman, op. cit, p 304.

129. Hankey: *Supreme Command*, vol. II, p 824. Roskill, *Hankey*, vol. I, p 501. Ullman, op. cit, p 327. Callwell: *Wilson*, vol. I, p 109. Memorandum by the General Staff for the War Cabinet on British Military Policy 1918–1919, 25th July 1918, WP 70. (Milner Papers, 126 AF 2).

130. Max Beloff: *Imperial Sunset*, vol. I, p 18. Stephen Roskill: *Naval Policy between the Wars*, vol. I (London 1968) p 219.

131. Eastern Committee, Minutes of 5th Meeting, 24th April 1918; 45th Meeting 19th December 1918 (Annex); 48th Meeting, 30th December 1918 (Annex).

132. Eastern Committee, Minutes of 41st Meeting, 5th December 1918 (Annex).

133. Eastern Committee, Minutes of 43rd Meeting, 16th December.

134. Roskill: *Hankey*, vol. I, pp 585, 611.

Chapter 4

135. James Eayrs: *In Defence of Canada* (Toronto 1964) vol. I, p 168.

136. ibid., p 330.

137. G. M. Gathorne-Hardy: *A Short History of International Affairs 1920–1939*, 4th ed. (London 1952) p 72.

138. W. K. Hancock: *Smuts: The Fields of Force 1919–1950* (London 1968) pp 129, 230.

139. 'General Staff Paper on the Military Liabilities of the Empire', 27th July 1920, C.I.D. Papers, 255-B, CAB 4/7.

140. 'Notes by General Staff for "The Imperial Cabinet"', 23 February 1921, C.I.D. Papers, 133-C, CAB 4/2.

141. War Cabinet 606A. F.C., 2nd Meeting, 1919.

142. See the Memorandum by Hankey of 23rd June 1931 summarizing the history of the Ten Year Rule, C.I.D. Papers, 1055-B.

143. B. R. Mitchell and Phyllis Deane: *Abstract of British Historical Statistics* (Cambridge 1962) pp 398–400. David Butler and Jennie Freeman: *British Political Facts 1900–1960* (London 1964) p 226.

144. Memorandum by Chancellor of the Exchequer of 17th May 1923 for the Sub-Committee on National and Imperial Defence, ND.33, CAB 16/47.

145. Keith Middlemas and John Barnes: *Baldwin: a Biography* (London 1969) pp 745–6, 969–73. For a re-interpretation of the East-Fulham by-election, widely but erroneously considered to have been fought on the issue of rearmament, see Richard Heller, 'East Fulham Revisited' in *Journal of Contemporary History*, vol. 6, no. 3, 1971.

146. Reprinted in H. A. Jones: *The War in the Air: the Story of the Part Played in the Great War by the Royal Air Force, Appendices* (Oxford 1937) pp 8–14.

147. 27th May 1921, C.I.D. 139th Meeting, CAB 2/3.

148. 31st October 1921, C.I.D., 147th Meeting, CAB 2/3.

149. C.I.D. Sub-Committee on Continental Air Menace Report, 26th April 1922, C.I.D. Papers, 106-A, CAB 3/3.

150. ibid.

151. Note by Lord Balfour on 29th May 1921, C.I.D. Papers 108-A, CAB 3/3.

152. 31st July 1922, C.I.D., 162nd Meeting, CAB 2/3.

153. 2nd August 1922, 163rd Meeting, CAB 2/3.

154. 9th March 1923, ND.1, CAB 16/47.

155. 10th May 1923, ND/9th Meeting, CAB 16/46.

156. Report of Sub-Committee on National and Imperial Defence (C.I.D.) November 1923. ND 68, CAB 16/47.

157. The Army's case was considered on 12th, 14th and 19th June 1923 (ND 12th, 13th and 14th Meetings) and disposed of in a memorandum by Salisbury on 30th June (ND 58, CAB 16/47).

158. See the paper put in by the Naval Staff, ND 12, and Beatty's defence of it on 17th and 19th April. (ND 3rd and 4th Meetings.)

159. See n. 156 above.

160. See n. 37 above.

161. For the sentiments of, in particular, Admirals Benson and Jones, U.S.N., see Stephen Roskill: *Naval Policy Between the Wars* (London 1968) vol. I, pp 54, 59, 64, 433–4. See also, H. and M. Sprout: *Towards a New Order of Sea Power* (Princeton 1940) pp 74–84.

162. Roskill: *Naval Policy between the Wars*, vol. I, p 291.

163. Beloff: *Imperial Sunset*, vol. I, p 343.

164. Memorandum by Sir Warren Fisher of 30th January 1934, DRC 12, CAB 16/109.

165. 3rd April 1924, C.I.D. 183rd Meeting, CAB 2/4.

166. C.I.D. Meetings of 5th January and 30th March 1925 (193rd and 198th Meetings.) CAB 2/4. It was agreed at this latter meeting that, although docking and fuelling facilities should be developed, 'there is no necessity . . . to make preparations involving additional expenditure for placing at Singapore, for a decisive battle in the Pacific, a British battlefleet . . . superior in strength, or at least equal, to the sea-going strength of Japan.'

167. Middlemas and Barnes: *Baldwin*, p 328. C.I.D., 236th Meeting, 5th July 1928, and C.I.D. Papers 819-B, CAB 2/5. On 8th November it was further decided that 'the question should no longer be brought up annually for review, but that it should be left to the discretion of Departments concerned to bring it to the notice of the Committee if and when they consider any modification desirable.'

168. 25th November 1926, C.I.D. 218th Meeting, CAB 2/4.

169. Memorandum by the C.I.G.S. of 25th March 1927 for the Defence of India Sub-Committee. DI 3, CAB 16/83.

170. DI 29, CAB 16/83.

171. DI 3rd and 4th Meetings, and Memoranda DI3 and 3a, CAB 16/83. The General Staff itself considered that conscription would be necessary, urging the necessity of throwing the Russians out of Afghanistan even at the price of 'a long and costly war'.

172. K. M. Pannikar: *Asia and Western Dominance* (London 1953) p 262.

173. Memorandum on Future Size of Regular Army by the General Staff, April 1923. ND 14, CAB 16/47.

174. Summary for Chiefs of Staff's Third Annual Review of Defence Policy 1928 by Hankey, 23rd July 1928. COS 140, CAB 53/14.

175. Elizabeth Monroe: *Britain's Moment in the Middle East* (London 1963) p 82.

176. ibid., p 126.

177. C.I.D., 195th Meeting, 13th February 1925; 196th Meeting, 19th February 1925; 200th Meeting, 22nd June 1925. Memorandum by CIGS for Cabinet. C.P. 116 (25).

178. Memorandum by Foreign Office for Chiefs of Staff Annual Review of Defence Policy 1926. COS 36, CAB 53/12.

179. Chiefs of Staff Sub-Committee Review of Imperial Defence, 22nd June 1926. COS 41, CAB 53/12.

180. E.g. in Revieps of Imperial Defence Policy, June 1928. COS 165, CAB 53/16; ('We cannot, in the early stages of a war, do much, except by naval means, to carry out our obligations under the Locarno Treaties') and July 1930, COS 247, CAB 53/21; ('We have received no instructions to work out plans in fulfilment of that guarantee, and in fact detailed plans have not been worked out. This country is in a less favourable position to fulfil the Locarno guarantees than it was, without any written guarantee, to come to the assistance of France and Belgium in 1914.').

181. See n. 138 above.

182. Cmd. 2768 (1926) p 30.

183. Eayrs, op. cit., p 23.

184. Quoted in a note by Lord Chatfield of 23rd June 1939. DP (P) 60.

Chapter 5

185. Chiefs of Staff Annual Review of Imperial Defence Policy. COS 295, CAB 53/22.

186. ibid.

187. Chiefs of Staff Report to the C.I.D. on the Situation in the Far East 22nd February 1932. COS 296, CAB 53/22.

188. Treasury Comments on COS 1932 Review, 11th March 1932. C.I.D. Papers 1087-B.

189. C.I.D. 255th Meeting, 22nd March 1932. Cabinet 19 (32) Concln. 2.

190. Marshal of the R.A.F., Sir John Slessor: *The Central Blue* (London 1956) p 161.

191. Imperial Conference 1937, *Summary of Proceedings* (London 1937) pp 14–16.

192. Foreign Affairs Committee of the Cabinet, 18th March 1938, quoted by Ian Colvin: *The Chamberlain Cabinet* (London 1970) p 109.

193. Report by Chiefs of Staff, August 1932, largely summarizing a Memorandum by the Overseas Defence Committee of 1928, C.I.D. 313-C (COS 298), CAB 53/22.

194. C.I.D., 256th Meeting, 9th June 1932. Cabinet 50 (32) Concln. 9.

195. See below p 118.

196. CP 218 (36).

197. COS 372, CAB 53/24.

198. Quoted by Arthur Marder: 'The Royal Navy and the Ethiopian Crisis of 1935–6', *American Historical Review*, XXV 5 (1970).

199. COS Report to the Defence Policy Requirements Committee, 16th September 1935. DPR 21, CAB 123.

200. CP 81 (36) and Cabinet 20 (36). They also warned (COS 442): 'If there is the smallest danger of being drawn into commitments which might lead to war with Germany, we ought at once to disengage ourselves from our present responsibilities in the Mediterranean, which have exhausted practically the whole of our meagre forces.' It was at this time that Baldwin informed Flandin: 'If there is one chance in a hundred that war will result from your police operation, I have not the right to involve England, because England is in no state to go to war.' (Middlemas and Barnes, *Baldwin* p 919.) In this he had the support of the opposition, whose spokesman on foreign affairs, Dr Hugh Dalton, told the House of Commons on 26 March: 'that public opinion in this country would not support, and certainly the Labour Party would not support, the taking of military sanctions or even of economic sanctions against Germany at this time, in order to put German troops out of the Rhineland.' House of Commons Debates, Fifth Ser., 340, col. 1454.

201. COS, 178th Meeting, 16th June 1936, quoted in Marder, loc. cit.

202. See n. 145.

203. Chiefs of Staff Annual Review of Defence Policy, 12th October 1933. COS 310, CAB 53/23.

204. C.I.D. 261st Meeting, 9th November 1933.

205. The minutes and memoranda of the Defence Requirements Committee are catalogued in the Cabinet Papers in the Public Records Office under CAB 109–111, Ser. DRC.

206. Defence Requirements. Sub-Committee Report, 28th February 1934, DRC 14.

207. DRC 7, DRC/6th and 12th Meetings.

208. DRC 12th Meeting. Chatfield refused to express an opinion but suggested that 'our proper advisers are the Air Ministry'.

209. DRC 7th Meeting.

210. For Liddell Hart's arguments against a 'continental strategy' see particularly *The British Way in Warfare* (London 1932) and *Europe in Arms* (London 1937). Chamberlain certainly read the latter, for he wrote a congratulatory note to the author and brought it to the attention of Hore-Belisha shortly after appointing him Secretary of State for War. B. H. Liddell Hart: *Memoirs* (London 1965) vol. I, p 386, and R. J. Minney: *The Private Papers of Hore-Belisha* (London 1960) p 54.

211. Disarmament Conference 1932—Ministerial Committee, Meeting of 3rd May, 1934. DC(M)(32), 41st Conclns.

212. COS 335, CAB 52/23.

213. 11th June 1934, DC(M)(32), 48th Conclns.

214. DC(M)(32) 120.

215. They were debated in Cabinet Committee for some five weeks, from 25th June until the end of July 1934. DC(M)(32), 50th–55th Conclns.

216. Meeting of 2nd July 1934, DC(M)(32), 52nd Conclns.

217. House of Commons Debates (Fifth Ser.) 292, col. 2339.

218. 'The Potential Air Menace to this Country from Germany'. Memorandum for Chiefs of Staff by the Air Staff, 12th June 1934. COS 341, CAB 53/24.

219. Richard M. Titmuss: *Problems of Social Policy*. (United Kingdom Official History of the Second World War, Civil Ser., ed. W. K. Hancock, London 1950) pp 4, 6. Sir Charles Webster and A. N. Frankland: *The Strategic Bombing of Germany*. (United Kingdom Official History of the Second World War, Military Ser., ed. J. R. M. Butler, London 1961) vol. I, pp 89–91.

220. House of Commons Debates (Fifth Ser.) 286, col. 2078.

221. Marshal of the R.A.F. Sir John Slessor: *The Central Blue*, pp 204–6. Slessor was Director of Plans in the Air Ministry from 1937 to 1940, and his memoirs are an essential source for this period.

222. Webster and Frankland: *The Strategic Bombing of Germany*, vol. I, pp 91–2.

223. 'Planning for War with Germany'; Report by the Chiefs of Staff to the Defence Plans (Policy) Sub-Committee of the C.I.D., DP (P) 1 & 2.

224. See especially Webster and Frankland, op. cit., pp 65–81, and Basil Collier: *The Defence of the United Kingdom* (London 1957) pp 28–35, 41–8, 63–75. Also Slessor, op. cit., pp 174–8.

225. Defence Requirements Committee Third Report, November 1935, DRC 37, CAB 111.

226. Statement on Defence 1936 (Cmd. 5107).

227. Defence Policy Requirements Committee Meeting of 14th January 1936, DPR (DR) 2nd Meeting.

228. CP 326 (36) and CP 334 (36). Chamberlain summarized his views in his diary entry for 25th October 1936. 'In my view . . . we had not the man-power to produce the necessary munitions for ourselves and perhaps, if the USA stood out, for our Allies, to man the enlarged Navy, the new Air Force, and a million men Army. . . . We should aim at an Army of 4 divisions plus 1 mobile division, and the necessary drafts to maintain its strength, and no more for overseas work. . . . Territorials should be kept for A.A. defence.' K. G. Feiling: *The Life of Neville Chamberlain* (London 1946) p 341. See also p 135 below.

229. It is significant that Hankey himself appears to have changed his mind in the course of 1937. In January 1936 he was urging Baldwin to support the Defence Requirements Committee's proposals for a Field Force, since the 'war can only be won by a combination that includes both France and Belgium' and if Britain did not help

Belgium, France would not. (Middlemas and Barnes: *Baldwin* p 904). 23rd November 1937, however, he wrote a Memorandum (CAB 21/53) pointing out (a) that France no longer expected Britain to provide aid on the scale hitherto proposed; (b) that Germany had guaranteed Belgian territory and in view of the vulnerability of the Ruhr and the Rhineland to an advance through Belgium would probably keep her word; (c) that the cost of aircraft and air defences had increased, and (d) that the increasing military commitments in Egypt, Palestine and the Far East might absorb all British military capacity. He recommended therefore that 'in the future the role of the Expeditionary Force should be to provide for the military requirements of the Empire and that the additional provision made in previous programmes to equip it for service on the Continent of Europe should be cancelled.'

230. 'Defence Expenditure in Future Years: Interim Report by Minister for Coordination of Defence.' 15th December 1937. CP 316 (37).

231. Cabinet Meeting of 22nd December 1937. Cabinet 49 (37). Eden did ask about the security of Belgium under the new arrangements. Hore-Belisha replied only that 'in view of our contribution by means of sea, air and finance, he did not think that the French ought to expect we could furnish an Army as well.'

232. CP 26 (38).

233. Webster and Frankland, op. cit., pp 75–7.

234. Chiefs of Staff Report on Staff Conversations with the French, 4th February 1938. CID Paper 1394-B. Minute by William Strang in FO 371/21653. Eden-Chamberlain, 31st January 1938. Premier 1/276. I am grateful to Mr John Lippincott for drawing my attention to these latter two documents.

235. Defence Requirements Committee, Third Report, 21st November 1935. DRC 37.

236. 'Comparison of the Strength of Great Britain with that of Certain Other Nations as at January 1938'. CID Paper 1366–B.

237. 'Chiefs of Staff Report on the Military Implications of German Aggression against Czechoslovakia', DP (P) 22.

238. See, e.g. *Documents on British Foreign Policy*, 3rd Ser., vol I, p 220.

Chapter 6

239. A. J. P. Taylor: *Origins of the Second World War* (London 1961) p 189.

240. R. Macleod and D. Kelly (ed.): *The Ironside Diaries* (London 1962) p 62.

241. 'Appreciation by the Chiefs of Staff Committee in the Event of War Against Germany', 4th October 1938. DP(P) 32.

242. Basil Collier: *The Defence of the United Kingdom*, p 65. Sir John Slessor: *The Central Blue* p 223.

243. Webster and Frankland, op. cit., p 100. See p 112 above.

244. 'Note on the Question of whether it would be to our military advantage to fight Germany now or to postpone the issue', by General Ismay, 22nd September 1938. CAB 21/544. Five days later the Chiefs of Staff reported: 'From the military point of view the balance of advantage is definitely in favour of postponement ... we are in bad condition to wage even a defensive war at the present time.' COS 772, 27th September 1938.

245. C.I.D., 341st Meeting, 15th December 1938.

246. Letter from Colonel W. Fraser of 22nd December 1938, Annex to DP(P) 42, 1st February 1939. The diary of

Major-General Henry Pownall, at the time Director of Military Operations in the War Office, sheds an interesting light on this document. The War Office had been pressing since the end of October for funds to bring the Field Force up to strength, and receiving evasive answers from the Cabinet. (31st October) 'P.M. and Halifax are going to Paris later this month and I fancy the pressure they will get from the French will be such that they may unwillingly have to agree to our proposals when they get back. I hope to "work" this a bit through our M.A. in Paris.' (14th November) 'I had Willie Fraser, M.A. in Paris, over during the week. . . . It would be highly improper for the G[eneral] S[taff] here to bring pressures to bear on the P.M. by French Ministers through the French G[eneral] S[taff] but I told Fraser to have a nice chat with Petitbon [*chef de cabinet* to Gamelin] and make hints, in the form of questions, that such questions might be raised during the discussions.' It seems reasonable to assume that the views reported by Fraser were those elicited by his 'hints'.

247. Memorandum by Halifax, 17th February 1939. DP(P) 47.

248. CP (316) 37 and CP (26) 38.

249. 'European Appreciation' by Chiefs of Staff Committee, 20th February 1939. DP(P) 44.

250. Cabinet Meeting of 2nd February 1939. Cabinet 5(39).

251. Cabinet Meeting of 22nd February 1939, Cabinet 8 (39). Public opinion also made itself felt, at this meeting, in rather a new role. Chamberlain, speaking of the weakness of the Field Force, said 'he thought that public opinion would become restive if the present position became known'; and Hore-Belisha said that 'up to this year there had been no Parliamentary pressure in regard to the Field Force, but pressure was now becoming evident.'

252. Cabinet 3 (39). A further jolt to the Cabinet had been administered by the rumour at the beginning of the year that Germany was about to launch a lightning attack on the Netherlands (CP 3 (39)). The comments by the Chiefs of Staff on such an eventuality showed a remarkable change from their attitude three months earlier. 'If we were compelled to enter such a war in the near future,' they reported 'we should be confronted with a position more serious than the Empire has ever faced before. The ultimate outcome of the conflict might well depend upon the intervention of other Powers, in particular of the U.S.A. . . . Nevertheless . . . failure to intervene would have such moral and other repercussions as would seriously undermine our position in the eyes of the Dominions and of the world in general. We might thus be deprived of support in a subsequent struggle between Germany and the British Empire.' (DP (P)43).

253. P. N. Mansergh: *Problems of External Policy*, 1919–1939 (Royal Institute of International Affairs Survey of Commonwealth Affairs, London 1939–52) pp 368–95. In South Africa the Prime Minister, Hertzog, intended to proclaim the country's neutrality without consulting Parliament. Smuts forced a division and defeated the Government by 80–67. South African participation in the war was thus decided by the votes of seven men.

254. R. J. Minney: *The Private Papers of Hore-Belisha*, p 193.

255. Cabinet Meeting of 29th March 1939, Cabinet 15 (39).

256. Cabinet 14 (39).

257. M. M. Postan: *British War Production* (U.K. Official History of the Second World War, Civil Ser. London 1952, p 345.
J. M. A. Gwyer and J. R. M. Butler: *Grand Strategy* vol. III (U.K. Official History of the Second World War, Military Ser. London 1964) p 547.

258. Cabinet Meeting of 20th March 1939, Cabinet 13 (39).

259. Strategic Appreciation Sub-Committee Meeting of 6th April 1939, S.A.C. 5th Meeting. Report by Chiefs of Staff Committee on 1st Stage of Anglo-French Staff Conversations, April 1939. DP (P) 56.

260. *Ironside Diaries*, p 78.

261. DP (P) 44.

262. DRC 12, CAB 16/109.

263. Feiling: *Chamberlain*, p 314. See n. 228 above.

264. 'Defence Expenditure in Future Years: Interim Report by Minister for Co-ordination of Defence'. 15th December 1937 CP 316 (37).

265. Postan, op. cit., p 12.

266. W. K. Hancock and M. M. Gowing: *British War Economy* (U.K. Official History of the Second World War, Civil Ser., London 1949) pp 115–16.

267. ibid., p 119.

268. Strategic Appreciation Sub-Committee, 6th April, SAC 4th Meeting.

269. CID 1305-B.

270. Appreciation by the Chiefs of Staff of the Situation in the Far East, June 1937, DP (P) 5.

271. Appreciation by the Chiefs of Staff of the Situation in the Event of War against Germany, 4th October 1938. DP (P) 32.

272. Quoted in F. S. Northedge: *The Troubled Giant* (London 1966) p 469.

273. Note on the Despatch of a Fleet to the Far East, by the Naval Staff, 5th April 1939. SAC 16.

274. Chiefs of Staff Report on the Situation in the Far East, 24th June 1939. DP (P) 61.

275. This was not realized by the Chiefs of Staff until 1937. See S. W. Kirby: *The War Against Japan, vol. I:*

The Fall of Singapore (U.K. Official History of the Second World War, Military Ser., London 1957) p 15.

276. J. R. M. Butler: *Grand Strategy* vol. II (U.K. Official History of the Second World War, Military Ser., London 1957) pp 492–3.

277. ibid., p 506.

278. loc. cit.

279. Randolph S. Churchill: *Winston S. Churchill* vol. II (London 1969) Companion, Part 3, p 1512.

280. J. M. A. Gwyer and J. R. M. Butler: *Grand Strategy* vol. III, p 367.

281. ibid., p 434.

282. James Eayrs: *In Defence of Canada: Appeasement and Rearmament* (University of Toronto Press, 1965) p 199.

283. Sir John Wheeler-Bennett: *George VI* (London 1964) p 460.

284. Butler: *Grand Strategy* vol. II pp 209–13.

285. Michael Howard: *The Mediterranean Strategy in the Second World War* (London 1968) passim.

Index